To my brother, Keir
Davidson, with profound
thanks for all his help and
encouragement in this and
other enterprises

GARDEN

contemporary exterior lighting

LIGHTING

James Davidson

WARD LOCK

First published in the United Kingdom in 1999 by
Ward Lock

Distributed in the United States by
Sterling Publishing Co. Inc.
387 Park Avenue South
New York NY 10016-8810

British Library Cataloguing-in-Publication Data
A catalogue record for this book is available from the British Library

ISBN 0-7063-7778-8

Design: Amzie Viladot Lorente
Illustrations: Inklink/Robin Harris

Printed and bound in Spain by Graficas Reunidas

Ward Lock
Illustrated Division
The Orion Publishing Group
Wellington House
125 Strand
London WC2R 0BB

CONTENTS

INTRODUCTION

When you light your home, you think about more than just the mundane business of extending daylight. This is, of course, why we include artificial light in our homes and into the environment in general – to give us more time by lengthening the useful part of the day – but this should not remain the only reason. From earliest times, people have tried to prolong the day so that they can work longer and be more productive or so that they can enjoy the time when they are not working. But we have progressed beyond the use of light for such limited purposes. No longer do we have to confine our activities to the period between dawn and dusk – we can go on for as long as we like.

In the early days, of course, it was considered a question of getting as much light as possible. The brighter the light and the more of it there was, the better, and the history of the development of artificial light is all to do with this – trying to make bigger and brighter light sources. From ancient oil lamps and tapers through candles and paraffin lamps with incandescent mantles, to gas and on to electricity in all its forms, finally arriving at fluorescent tubes and the high-powered halogen and discharge lamps used by sports stadia and the like, the ultimate goal was to find a way to make the most light for the least cost and with the least fuss. The switch on the wall, turning on that bright, central light bulb, originally had a magic we can now only guess at. It must have seemed fantastic – the ultimate achievement.

By now, however, we have learned to temper our enthusiasm somewhat and to put as much – or more – thought into the quality of the artificial light we use as we have done into its quantity. We now want to understand exactly why we want light in a certain place and to discover how much light we need and of what sort. This is certainly true in professionally designed environments. The business of lighting design is much more to do with introducing suitable light than with just providing large amounts of it. For many in the industry, this is a precise science, particularly when it comes to lighting working environments or those places, such as supermarkets or restaurants, where the quality of the lighting can be directly linked to sales and thus to the success of the whole enterprise.

I would hope that non-professionals will achieve this awareness too. We may know what lighting can do to impress and inspire us at work and as we go about our everyday affairs, but we do not always see it in the context of our personal lives. We are surrounded by the lighting effects used in commercial and public places – the self-aggrandizement

A garden is not just for daytime – this wittily lit corner is ideal for relaxing after a hard day's gardening.

of corporate headquarters; the illumination of public buildings and historic monuments for the benefit of visitors and sightseers; even, occasionally, the thoughtful lighting of public spaces in our towns – but only slowly are we recognizing that we can adapt and apply similar effects to our own, domestic, situations. Reducing them in scale, we can make them work in our gardens just as well as they do in the town park. If we are lucky enough to have a garden on the same scale as the town park, so much the better, of course, but any size will do.

Your motives will be different and your approach will be far more intuitive, but many of you will already have begun to appreciate the difference between quality and quantity. Your home may already be well lit in terms of the uses to which you put the available space, and you may have a good and clear understanding of the principles of interior lighting.

I have already dealt with lighting for the home in *The Complete Home Lighting Book*, in which I touch only briefly on the garden and the outside of the house. Now, however, I want to take you outdoors altogether and into your garden – into a part of your home that is often neglected after dark. I hope to encourage you to look at your house and garden as two aspects of a single entity, both of which can benefit from artificial lighting.

To achieve this end, we need to start at the beginning and to cover some of the basic principles and technical details of the subject and, most importantly, to encourage you to consider both light and your garden. Exterior lighting is a different business altogether from interior lighting, not only in the detail but in the reasons we attempt it at all.

Exterior lighting is, in many ways, simple enough in concept, but it can be difficult to get right. It requires a different way of thinking, being less to do with practicalities and much more to do with just having fun. Perhaps too few people are willing to do things just for pleasure, and certainly the people who

are interested in lighting their gardens are in a minority, and many of those who do put lights outside do so without giving sufficient thought to what is possible.

In many parts of the world, particularly in Britain and northern Europe, gardens are largely regarded as something to be enjoyed only and exclusively during daylight hours. Whether it is in the town or the countryside, the garden is usually regarded as being for moments of relaxation – it is a piece of private landscape in which we can escape from the world.

There is more to lighting your garden than putting up a floodlight, and this bold installation is as exciting to look at as it is useful to see by.

Many of us will, in fact, have organized it with exactly that use in mind. Often, even in modestly sized gardens, some thought will have been given to the overall design, and features will have been arranged so that they can be looked at from specific viewing positions to provide the best angles. Usually these vantage points will, themselves, be in the garden, and it is rare for the view from inside the house to be taken into account. The garden as a 'picture' is, in any case, an idea that is reserved largely for daylight hours. After dark we tend to ignore the outside, but in so doing, we pass up the chance to have a quite different, and often a more dramatic, 'picture'.

Even in countries where sitting in the garden is regarded as a normal occurrence only on summer days, there are many times throughout the year when it is possible to sit outside and enjoy the garden late into the evening. Even in winter a garden can be a beautiful sight. A light fall of snow can transform a dull winter landscape into a vision that, if lit at night, can be quite breathtaking. The expression 'an extra

room' is used increasingly to describe the garden, but the term is generally considered to apply to a day room. Even among those who do use their gardens at night, providing lighting there is often considered a luxury and not done at all, or, at best, is carried out in an ill-conceived and partial way. Too often, a single floodlight is placed high on a wall and thought to be enough. Those people who regularly cook and eat outside will probably have installed some kind of lighting for that purpose, but it is still comparatively rare for the rest of the garden to be lit for any other purpose than to provide security or to facilitate access.

It makes no difference if your garden is large or small, has hard or soft features, or is modern or traditional in style – putting in light makes an enormous difference. If the garden is large enough to wander around, specific walks and discrete areas can be lit to create different moods and moments, which may entice you further along a path or draw you into an unexpectedly secluded spot. Irrespective of the complexity of the layout of your garden, light can enhance and dramatize the best aspects and features. Light can create illusions, and it can be a feature in its own right. Modern systems and fittings make possible some quite startling effects through, for example, the use of colour and movement or by combining light with water.

There are practical considerations, of course – such as lighting for access and to discourage intruders – but garden lighting is, on the whole, a theatrical business, and you should think of it as an opportunity to let your imagination have free rein. This is lighting for play time. There are fewer needs for task lighting once you get outside and far greater scope for accent and adventure. A good lighting scheme can transform the daylight scene, enabling practical night-time use without compromising beauty and mystery.

Lighting up the night-time garden is largely done for recreational reasons rather than practical ones. The garden is intended to be looked at and the lighting is used to create a spectacle. Of all the places around the house, the garden is often where we have done the most work and spent the most time planning and dreaming. We may have made long trips to garden centres and put in many hours of back-breaking toil to make those dreams come true. But when darkness falls, we go indoors, more often than not, drawing the curtains to shut it out. In addition to creating this extra room outside, we should not forget the view from the house. We do not have to be in the garden in order to appreciate its beauty. When we provide the correct balance of light indoors and out, the garden can still be seen through the windows when it is dark, just as we might enjoy looking at it from indoors on a sunny afternoon.

Subtle pools of light in carefully chosen places allow this garden to come alive after dark and make the 'extra room' doubly useful.

Gardens are ideal for using the lighting as a feature in itself where mere illumination is of secondary importance.

Without some understanding of the special problems that exterior lighting presents, it is, however, all too easy to get it wrong. It is now widely accepted that no matter how good your interior décor, the careless use of light can destroy the effect you may have worked long and hard to achieve. We know, for example, that the colour and intensity of a light source can completely alter the colour of the paint that is applied to the walls and can make or break the atmosphere we have carefully set out to create. This effect can also be true of the outside.

Yet so much can be done with lighting to make the garden interesting and visually stimulating at night, whatever its size and complexity. There is no space so small or so confined that it cannot be lit to good effect. A small town courtyard can benefit every bit as much as an extensive, rambling country

garden, whether you wish to be out in it or to observe it from indoors. Your scheme does not have to be grand and expensive; you can achieve a great deal in just a small space and on quite a modest budget.

I hope to inspire you to think of your garden not just as somewhere you do the gardening or sunbathe on hot, sunny summer days, but as a place where you can look for recreation in the true sense of the word and where you can enjoy the space in all its aspects and at all hours of the day and night. This book is intended to show you something of what is possible, to enable you to set up interesting and attractive visual effects, and to help you create the atmosphere best suited to you and your garden. You will have put a lot of thought and, probably, hard work into creating your garden, and I want to encourage you to stay out there after dark and to enjoy the fruits of your efforts after the work has, necessarily, got to stop.

My aim is, first, to encourage you to look at your garden and the potential for lighting it and then to guide you through the process from the very first inspiration, through the analysis of your wants and needs, the planning of a specific scheme to suit your garden and your purse, and on to organizing the final installation.

This is not a book about designing your garden; it is about making the best and fullest use of the garden that you have designed. My aim is to inspire you as much as I am hoping to guide you, although I would stress that much of what follows is my opinion and does not constitute hard and fast rules. You may well disagree with me, in which case I will be glad to have opened the debate.

One last word at this stage: without powerful floodlighting, you will be unable to illuminate your whole garden nor, whatever you do, will you be able make your garden look as it does during the day. But you should not want to do this. The object of installing lighting is not to simulate the sun but, rather, to create a new and special, night-time garden. Those of you who wish to extend the use of your garden into the evening should be aware of the difference that light can make to what you think your garden looks like and learn how to look at it in a different way. It will not appear as an homogeneous whole, as it does during the day, but as a series of individual lit features, which should combine to make a new and quite different picture of your garden.

These copper tubes are more sculpture than lighting, despite the fact that this may be their main purpose. Features like these can add another dimension to your garden both by day and by night.

Note

Throughout this book British terminology has been used and a mains voltage of 240v has been assumed. In many other European countries mains voltage is 220v while, in the United States, it is 110v (doubled for large appliances). If in doubt, you should always consult a qualified electrician.

the TECHNICALITIES

A good example of detail lighting using twin up-spotlights with colour filters.

This chapter covers the technical aspects of light; it will not, I hope, be correspondingly dull. Although my aim is to inspire and encourage, there is, inevitably, a certain amount of technical information that you will need to know. In this chapter, therefore, are some explanations of technical terms and definitions of light, equipment and accessories that will be used in later chapters. This chapter is intended to provide a painless introduction to the technicalities of light and its use and to equip you with the knowledge and the tools that you will need to design a lighting scheme yourself and to carry your ideas forward.

I should stress here, however, that I do not advocate the do-it-yourself approach. You should never confuse 'lighting' with 'electricity'; they are entirely separate things. However, you will need electricity to operate your lighting system and will, in consequence, have to understand something about it just on a theoretical level. The terms that are, I believe, necessary for you to know are described in this chapter but electricity itself is a subject and an area of expertise on its own, especially when it is used outdoors, and it should be considered beyond the reach of even the most competent D-I-Y enthusiast. Quite apart from the inherent dangers, there are parts of the world where no electrical installation can be carried out without due certification or you risk invalidating your insurance policy. In parts of the United States, for example, you would be unable to sell your house without such certification. So just don't do it. Before anybody electrocutes him- or herself and reaches for a lawyer, I say now – leave electricity to a qualified electrician.

Good use is made of old and new technologies here, with electricity making the tree a strong focal point and candles giving a softening balance alongside.

This luminaire is a compact spotlight, the light source being a small 12v lamp with a lens that concentrates the beam.

Understanding the light source

Because lighting has its own jargon, it is important to understand the terms that professionals use:

• *A luminaire is the whole thing: lamp, lamp holder, body, shade and so on.*

• *A lamp is the light source and consists of the bulb, filament and appropriate fitting.*

• *A lamp holder is the device into which a lamp is plugged.*

• *Light is the beam or glow of light emitted by a lamp.*

Definitions

As with most areas of human endeavour, lighting has spawned its own jargon, much of which is quite meaningless to the uninitiated. In fact, it is not the vocabulary itself that is the problem, because it has, like any specialist language, evolved to make life easier for the initiated. The problem is the limit of that initiation – just how many, or few, people are familiar with the words in question. The vocabulary is not a jealously guarded secret, but it is important that you become familiar with the professional terminology, so that we are all speaking the same language. Further difficulties are caused by local usage – for example, an American electrician may well use a different expression from a British one to describe something. Therefore, to avoid any misunderstandings, the most important terms are defined here.

Unlike lighting inside the house, outdoor lighting depends largely on the use of spotlights and floodlights, and almost all exterior lighting will be done using projectors. Already, in that one sentence, I have used three technical terms with specific meanings: spotlight, floodlight and projector. Although these are probably all words you know, their precise meanings are obvious to me, but it would be unsafe for me to assume that you share my understanding – that is, that we agree fully on the specific meaning of even the terms you recognize.

The words people use to describe lighting can be confusing. The great range of lighting types and applications – from the industrial to the domestic, from retail environments to the theatre – makes this inevitable. In addition, each area of specialism has its own particular forms of lighting and its own terminology. Fortunately, there are sufficient overlaps and similarities to lay down some general rules, which will at least serve for our purposes. Most people would regard a lamp as something into which you insert a bulb and which becomes a light. Professionals tend to say that a luminaire is something into which you insert a lamp and which gives light. For the purposes of this book, I am going to use the professional terms because, once you have the hang of them, they will avoid all danger of confusion. Not everyone may agree with my definitions, but they are as close to a standard as I can get.

One of the most important areas to understand is the distinction between light, lights and lighting. The differences between the three are absolutely fundamental and until we get them clear in our minds we will probably find ourselves talking at cross-purposes. It may, on the face of it, seem like stating the obvious, but light is not the same thing as lighting and certainly not the same as lights. In summary, light is what we play with to create lighting, and in the process of doing this we have to use lights.

It is, however, the nature and form of light that makes everything work; all the rest is secondary. Having distinguished between light, lights and lighting, we will, therefore, use 'light source' instead of 'light' and 'luminaires' instead of 'lights'.

The Light Source

The light source is the most important part of any lighting scheme: it is the part that actually produces the light we are going to use. From a design point of view, the light source is the primary part of the

Watts and volts

To the non-scientist, electricity can be a troublesome concept to grasp, and it is beyond the scope of this book. However, it will be useful to define the common terms in as straightforward a way as possible, in an attempt to avoid confusion. A scientist may not be entirely happy with these definitions, but so be it – they shouldn't need them.

- *A volt (V) is the unit of electromotive force by which current is measured.*

- *A watt (W) is the unit of power by which the output of a lamp is determined.*

- *A lumen (lm) is the unit of light by which the output of a lamp is measured.*

- *Lux (lx) is the number of those lumens per square metre.*

equation and the part that will be considered before anything else. When we ask ourselves, 'How do I want to light this tree?' it is the light source that is the first consideration. It is the nature and form – the quality and quantity of its output – that will establish the shape, the size and the colour of the tree and create the feel, the atmosphere – in short, the effect that illuminating the tree will have on the viewer. This is the light – the light source, and that means, effectively, the lamp.

A traditional coach lamp, which has a decorative body fitted with a common household all-round-glow lamp.

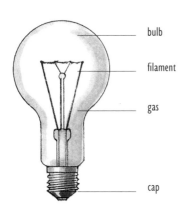

bulb

filament

gas

cap

A tungsten filament lamp.

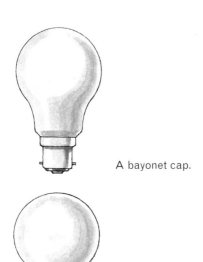

A bayonet cap.

An Edison screw.

Most of us talk about light bulbs, but professionals would tend to call these lamps. This is because a lamp is made up of several components, only one of which is the bulb.

From now on, we will be using the word 'lamp', so it is important for you to know what is meant by this. A lamp consists of a bulb and a cap.

- A bulb is the glass envelope that contains the filament or gas. The glass can be clear, frosted or coloured; it can be globular, conical or tubular; and it can be with or without a reflective finish. All of these are bulbs.

- A cap is the means by which the lamp is fitted into the lamp holder. All bulbs have at least one cap; some have two, one at each end of a tube.

So, it is the combination of the bulb, its contents and the cap that makes a lamp, the light source.

The word lamp is also used in other ways, most often in conjunction with a qualifying noun – coach lamp, carriage lamp and lamp-post, for example. This is not as perverse as it sounds, but because these terms

A simple body, not much more than a lamp holder, carries a mains-voltage PAR spot lamp.

are historic and traditional it would be pointless to attempt to invent new ones just for the sake of it. You should recognize them easily by their context.

The lamp is, therefore, what produces the light, but the form that light takes depends on other factors, and it is these factors that will determine which lamp you chose for a specific job. Interior lighting, particularly in domestic situations, makes much use of the all-round-glow type of lamp. Outdoors lighting, on the other hand, is most often done with projectors.

Projectors

Projectors are lamps that are designed to throw – that is, to project – a beam of light in one direction only, although the width of the beam is variable. A narrow beam is called a spotlight; a wide one is called a floodlight. These names are often shortened to spot and flood.

The variations of these beam widths are what enable us to create the effects we want, and

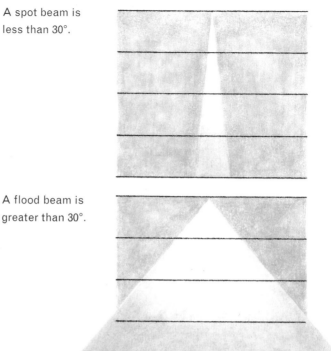

A spot beam is less than 30°.

A flood beam is greater than 30°.

- A spotlight (spot) is a beam of light of an angle less than 30°.

- A floodlight (flood) is a beam of light of an angle greater than 30°.

In fact, there are more than just two widths, and manufacturers often indicate the beam width on the packaging of the lamps, usually using standard initials:

- NS (narrow spot), also known as a pin spot, is a beam between 6 and 12°.

- SP (spot) is a beam up to 30°.

- FL (flood) is a beam between 30 and 45°.

- WFL (wide flood) is a beam of about 60°.

- VWFL (very wide flood) is a beam up to 80°.

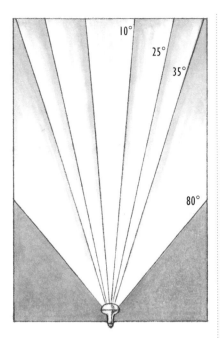

The range of beam widths.

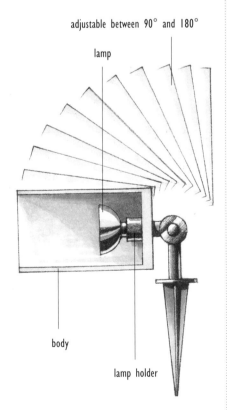

adjustable between 90° and 180°

lamp

body

lamp holder

A typical spike-mounted spotlight.

it is important that they be understood. But remember that the beam width is not just a matter of the spread of light that is produced; it will also have an effect on the amount of light that is produced. A very narrow beam will project its light over a greater distance than a very wide beam even if both beams are of the same wattage.

There are two basic types of projector lamp: those with an internal reflector and those with an external reflector. You will recognize the first type as the cone-shaped lamps used around the home in spotlight clusters and the like, and as the chunkier PAR lamps (see below). Almost without exception, these are mains voltage. Some PAR lamps are low voltage, designed for specific tasks, as I mention below. The second type, which is becoming more commonly used in the home, are the halogen lamps with dichroic reflectors, which are nearly always low voltage, most often 12V.

These and the PAR lamps are the two projectors most often used in domestic garden lighting schemes. Low-voltage lighting will, of course, need transformers, so it can be more costly to install, but the lamp life expectancy is much greater than it is with mains voltage lamps, and they do use less electricity. It is simply a choice between higher installation cost with low running costs and cheaper installation cost with high running costs.

PAR Lamps

Available as both tungsten-filament and halogen, parabolic aluminized reflector (PAR) lamps are robust, internal reflector lamps with moulded lenses that focus the light into a specific beam. They nearly always need mains voltage, with outputs of between 75W and 150W for the PAR38 and up to 300W for the PAR56.

One form of PAR56 lamp is designed specifically for use underwater, when the water disperses the heat generated by the high wattage. These are available as low voltage as well as mains voltage.

Halogen Capsule Lamps

Neat and compact halogen capsule lamps have astonishing output for their size. In their capsule form they are all-round-glow lamps, but they are most often used in conjunction with a reflector, which turns them into projectors. They use low voltage, 12V or 24V, and range from 10W to 100W in output. A significant point is that the amount of light they produce per watt is a great deal more than their tungsten-filament counterparts.

DICHROIC REFLECTOR LAMPS

These are essentially the same as capsule lamps with reflectors, but the reflector is 'built in', so that they make up a complete unit, often with a glass front as well. The dichroic reflector is a multi-faceted glass bowl, coated in such a way that it reflects light forwards but conducts heat backwards. These lamps have a long life expectancy – up to five times that of many tungsten-filament lamps. Halogen lamps are also favoured by many because of the 'sparkle' in the light they produce.

All-round-glow

This is not, as far as I am aware, an accepted technical expression. By it, I mean those lamps that do not throw a beam of light in any particular direction on their own and that, are, therefore, different from projectors. The standard domestic 'light-bulb' is such a lamp, but they can take many forms. These standard domestic lamps are not used much, if at all, for outdoor lighting, and the most usual place to find an all-round-glow lamp is in bulkhead luminaires and bollards, and even here, they are fast being replaced with long-life, low-energy, compact fluorescents. Paradoxically, a common position for an all-round-glow lamp is in conjunction with an external reflector – when it becomes a projector! The most powerful projectors are, in fact, those that use this combination, and a light-house is an extreme example of this use.

One other factor to consider in the definition of a lamp is the means by which it generates light. Most indoor lamps will be incandescent or fluorescent, particularly for domestic use. Outdoors, a third category is often used – the high-pressure discharge lamp. The quality, colour and sheer quantity of the light produced by high-pressure discharge lamps is fundamentally important to outdoor lighting – indeed any lighting – and they are discussed in detail on pages 36–37.

Transformers

All low-voltage luminaires will need a transformer. Many come with one built in. Alternatively, you can use a single, remote transformer to run several luminaires. The number of lights that can run off one transformer is determined by the capacity of the transformer and the power of the lamps. For example, a 100VA transformer can run 5 × 20w lamps or 2 × 50w lamps. Outdoors it is often preferable to use high-capacity transformers to run groups of luminaires. The only thing to be careful of is voltage drop. Your contractor will know about this and will be able to advise you on the most appropriate set-up for your circumstances.

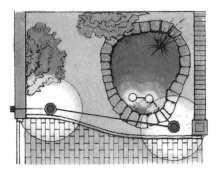

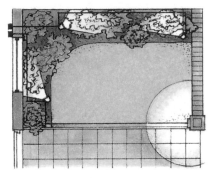

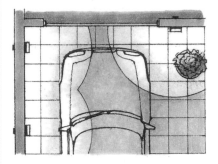

ALTERNATIVE CIRCUITS

Three examples of wiring set-ups are shown here. The first has a single, large transformer running a number of luminaires. The second has two smaller transformers, an arrangement that gives greater flexibility. The third set-up uses luminaires with integral transformers.

The traditional street lamp brought into the garden; this is no different in essence from the gas and early electric street lights of yesteryear.

Luminaires

The luminaire is the object that carries the lamp holder, which holds the lamp. It may be designed to produce an unfocused pool of light, or it may be designed to concentrate the beam by using a combination of focusing lenses and reflectors, in which case it becomes a projector. It may be intended to be hidden and designed to conceal the source of the beam, or it may be decorative in its own right and intended to be looked at. Whatever the case, each luminaire will have been originally designed to perform a specific function. Nevertheless, each one will be made up of certain common components, and it is important that you know something about these, or problems can arise. You may have already come up against that moment when you bought the lamp with the Edison screw (ES) cap when what you wanted was the bayonet clip (BC) cap – I have. Knowing your luminaire is important.

A coach lamp fitted with frosted, or
opal, glass to give a gentle glow,
avoiding hard shadows.

A modern design on an old theme,
this is a hybrid between a bollard and
a coach lamp.

A luminaire is made up of the lamp holder and the body.

- The lamp holder is the device into which you plug the lamp – beware, it will be designed to take only one specific type of cap and they are not interchangeable.

- The body is what holds the lamp holder, which takes the form of a box or tube (square or round) – whatever is appropriate to the intended use, in fact. This body may have accessories – add-on bits, such as anti-glare cowls or directional louvres or other devices, which are intended to affect the spread and throw of the beam. Many luminaires, especially those with enclosed body, will have maximums for the lamp – you should refer to the packaging.

These accessories are more important than you might think, and it is worth considering them in more detail.

Lenses

A lens is usually used only in the sort of luminaire that has a built-in reflector and carries an all-round-glow lamp. The most obvious place you get this combination is in the headlights of your car. Lenses will make a wide beam narrow or even change its shape altogether – for example, turning a circle of light into an ellipse. This can be useful if you want to light tall trees or long walls.

A filter is a specialized form of lens. Filters will not affect the shape of the beam, but they can change its colour or its focus. PAR lamps have such lenses as a main feature.

Cowls

More often than not, cowls are rigid. They are designed to cover three-quarters of the business end of the luminaire if it is round, or three sides of it if it is square. They are intended to prevent light spill from getting into your eyes or to send the light in a particular direction.

One useful form of cowl, though, sadly, rare outside the doors of a theatre or away from a film unit, are barn-doors. This is a rather silly name, I grant you, but it is a good enough description of what they do. Barn-doors are flaps on four side of a luminaire, which can be adjusted to cut the light off, to a greater or lesser extent, in any of those four directions. They will not cut out all the light, but they will do enough to prevent it getting where you don't want it. It will do this with a hard edge, which can be a considerable advantage. The barn-door originated in the theatre, where it is still widely used. In the garden they are invaluable for preventing light spill, as, for example, when you want to light a row of low shrubs but not the trees behind them.

Louvres

A slightly different idea from cowls or barn-doors, louvres perform a similar job. They are used to prevent light from going in an unwanted direction. A good example of this would be when they are fitted to wall-mounted path-lighters, where you want to prevent any light from shining forwards or upwards (which would create glare) but want to make sure that most of it goes downwards to do the job of lighting the path.

A special form of louvre takes the form of a shallow honeycomb. This is often fitted to uplighters

This path-lighter uses all-round louvres to direct the light in a downwards direction only.

to prevent side glare in any direction, thereby rendering the light source almost invisible.

A luminaire, therefore, consists of all these things – lamp, lamp holder, body, accessory and so on.

The names for describing luminaires are generally descriptive and are more readily understood than those used for the lamps, but the common types are listed below for easy reference. There are two categories for the names of luminaires: one is descriptive of what it does, and the other is descriptive of what it is. It is important to remember,

A good range of accessories is available if you know where to look; here are various louvres, cowls, lenses and barn doors.

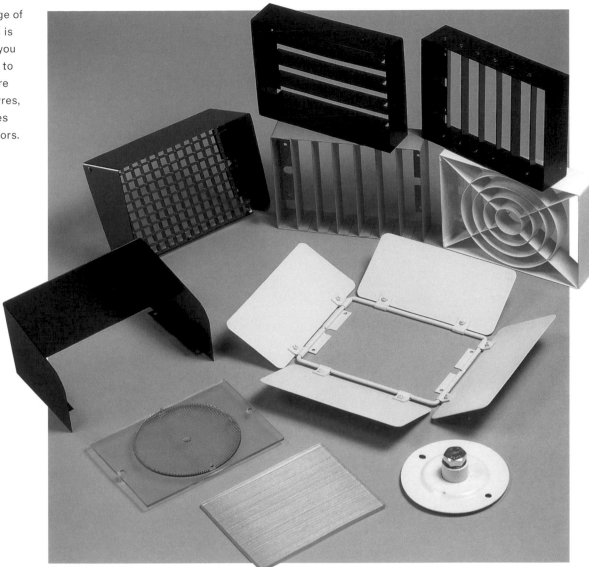

however, that the same luminaire can be used to perform more than one task. The difference between an uplighter and a downlighter may be simply the way up it is used – an uplighter turned upside down becomes a downlighter. In the first group – defined by function – we are not so much describing objects as we are discussing concepts. If, for example, we want a light to shine upwards, we will describe it as an uplighter, irrespective of the shape or form of the luminaire or what it was originally intended to do. Thinking in this way will help us to select the correct luminaire for the job.

Forms of Light

So far we have looked at the hardware – the light source, luminaires and their bolt-on bits – but we have not discussed light in its abstract form. Throughout the book, I will be describing light in terms that may not be familiar to you, and it will be useful to define these briefly here.

First, however, it might be helpful to know something of the way electric light is made. In most domestic use, both indoors and out, it will be by one of two ways: incandescence and fluorescence.

Types of luminaire

Some luminaires are described by function:

- *An uplighter is a luminaire that is intended to shine upwards only; it is often mounted on a spike so that it can be stuck in the ground.*

- *A recessed uplighter is a luminaire that is designed to be buried in the ground.*

- *A wall-washer is often a recessed uplighter fitted with a cowl or a lens or some other means of directing and spreading the beam over a wide, but controlled, area.*

- *A downlighter is a luminaire that is intended to shine downwards only.*

- *A path-lighter is a luminaire that is designed specifically to illuminate paths, steps, terraces or driveways.*

- *A recessed path-lighter is a path-lighter that is fitted at ground level.*

There are, however, some luminaires whose names describe the object rather than the function:

- *A bollard is an upright post with a built-in lamp that is mainly used to illuminate car parks and larger driveways but also sometimes decks and terraces.*

- *A bulkhead, a term borrowed from the sea, is a luminaire fitted to a wall or other vertical surface to provide practical, all-round light.*

- *A coach lamp or carriage lamp is a wall-mounted luminaire designed to imitate the oil lamps that were fitted to the horse-drawn coaches of earlier times and that are now most often used to illuminate entrances, particularly front doors.*

- *A lantern is a pendent luminaire or a luminaire that is fitted to the top of a post to make a lamp-post.*

Incandescence

Incandescent light is produced by passing an electric current through a wire filament. This makes it glow white hot, thus producing light. Incandescent light takes two forms that we need to know about – the standard tungsten-filament lamp and the halogen lamp. The first of these, the tungsten-filament lamp, is the ubiquitous light bulb, of which one most useful form for the garden is the PAR projector (see page 20).

The halogen lamp (see page 20) is the low-voltage lamp, which we use mostly in the forms of dichroic reflectors and capsule lamps.

Fluorescence

Fluorescence results from causing something to absorb invisible radiation and to emit visible radiation. We are familiar with the fluorescent tube and, increasingly, with the 'energy-saving' compact fluorescent, which is now often used instead of tungsten-filament lamps, especially outdoors. These fluorescent lamps are low-pressure discharge lamps. Another type of fluorescent light is neon, but this is beyond the scope of this book.

High-pressure Discharge

A more important variation as far as garden lighting is concerned is the high-pressure discharge lamp. Such lamps as mercury vapour, metal halide or sodium discharge are forms of high-pressure discharge lamp. They are usually high-output lamps, but what is most significant about them is their effect on colour, which we will consider further on pages 35–7.

Describing Light

The abstract idea of light is often described in two main ways – as practical light and as accent light.

- Practical light is intended primarily to illuminate a task or human function, and it covers such things as light to eat by at the barbecue or light by which to see your way around your garden.

- Accent light is intended primarily to be decorative. It is used to illuminate an object and to create features that are dramatic and exciting to look at.

The expression ambient light is used to describe the quality and quantity of light within a given space, which is created by the sum of practical and accent light. Ambient light can be either direct or indirect.

Direct light shines directly on to an object or surface. Indirect light, however, is reflected off something – a wall for example – or it is light that deliberately creates reflections on water – mirror lighting – or that illuminates something secondary to its main focus. Much of the ambient light in a space will be indirect light – that is, light that is spilled from luminaires doing a different primary job.

Another way in which we describe light is by its colour temperature. The effect of any lighting scheme will be a product of this as much as of anything else. When we use such terms as a 'warm, soft light' or a 'harsh, cold light' we are referring to the colour temperature.

This temperature is the wavelength of the light emitted by a lamp, which is expressed as degrees Kelvin ($°K$); this is discussed further on pages 35–6.

We will be looking at all these things in greater detail in subsequent chapters, but for now the most important thing to know is that all lighting design is a balance between light and dark. It is not enough to know only about how to make light and point it at

Direct light.

Indirect light.

something. We have to understand, and be able to use, the value of its by-product, shadow, and the difference between that and darkness. Shadow is created by the presence of light; darkness can be defined as the absence of light.

It is all to do with the balance between light and dark and that brings us to the very fundamentals of design itself.

the PRINCIPLES of LIGHTING DESIGN

The epitome of accent light – a compact spotlight shining up through the foliage of nearby planting.

This book is about lighting your garden – that part of your house that is increasingly known as the extra room. The expression 'the extra room' is significant because it helps to define how we think about our gardens. Many people regard their gardens as work places, where they grow vegetables and fruit for the table. Some people may not really think about their garden at all – it is just a patch of land outside the house and somewhere to park the car. However, because you are reading this book, it is probably safe to assume that you think rather more of your garden than that.

We can keep the garden as a strictly daytime place, or we can take a bold step and stay out there after dark, using the garden as a place to relax, to entertain and so on, just as we use the reception rooms indoors – and we wouldn't dream of restricting the use of an indoor room on the basis of the time of day, except in the largest of houses. If we are going to use our gardens in the evening, we will need light, and if that light is not going to be utilitarian, we will have to think about it from the point of view of design. Design comes into it not only because you want to do it properly and safely but also because it is a part of your home. This lighting is not something that will be done in isolation: it will be integral to the style of garden you have and how you intend to

use it, and it will reflect your personality and affect the way you and your visitors feel about your home – is it attractive or not?

Lighting design, as any other practical function, has a theory and a practice. The theory covers what light is and how it affects our moods and responses. The practice covers your choice of luminaires and lamps and where you use them. Remember that finding the right lamp for a particular task is governed by more than just aesthetic qualities; factors such as economy and value for money are equally important.

Lighting design is all about the creation of atmosphere. Here an intimate feel is achieved by using concealed electric lighting and having a candle as a focal point.

These ethereal glass rods serve to illuminate the surrounding plants and give a visually stimulating accent light that adds interest to the garden as a whole.

Professional lighting designers will be aware of these considerations, particularly since many of the projects they undertake involve efficiency and the need to keep running costs low. Knowing how to use light and how to choose the right light for the job is essential for anyone who is interested in their environment and in seeking to make the best of it, and this is no less true outdoors than it is indoors, even if it is largely recreational.

Analysing Light

In the previous chapter we explored what light is and how it is made. Now we need to understand the forms light can take, and also what influences these forms and how we can manipulate them. In short, we need to know how we can use them in the garden to achieve our dreams. Although we use some common lamp types both inside and out, lighting

A standard PAR 38 lamp in a simple holder illuminates the pergola and the path. Its position may not be ideal since it is likely to produce glare to passers-by, but it performs its function well otherwise.

outside will, generally, need more powerful lamps and this means that we will make use of one or two specialized lamps. It is often the case that more powerful lamps are used to illuminate outdoor spaces than you would dream of using indoors – lamps with up to 300W output and more are regularly used in lighting architecture and public spaces, and they are not unknown in domestic gardens. After all, an average room will be about 3.4m (11ft) high, whereas even a modest tree will be at least 6m (20ft) high.

The means of producing the light for outdoors differ as well. While indoors you would normally expect to find incandescent and low-pressure discharge lamps – the common tungsten filament and halogen lamps and fluorescent tubes and their compact versions – outside we also meet such exotic things as metal halide, mercury discharge and other high-pressure discharge lamps.

A number of small, well-placed lights are always better than a few very bright ones.

This solar-powered fluorescent defines the practical as opposed to the decorative. It makes a very useful light source but not one, perhaps, that you would want to look at.

The essential difference between all these is how much of the spectrum is included in the light they produce – the colour of the light, and the colours it can distinguish. This is an important feature of lighting outdoors, and it is discussed in detail later. First, however, let us consider the quality of the light we are bringing to our garden.

Quality or Quantity

The amount of light you introduce into an environment and the quality of that light are critical to the result you achieve, but, as with so many things in life, so with light – more is not necessarily better. It is all too easy to overdo it and destroy the very thing you are trying to create. Even those who have not visited football and other games stadia will be aware of the fantastic banks of floodlights, which are placed high in the air to get as much light on to the pitch as possible and to prolong the illusion of daylight. In terms of quantity, this is fine. In terms of quality, however, it is far from being so. The expression 'lit up like a football pitch' is not one most of us would wish applied to our gardens. Unless you want to play sports at night, I would suggest that you should be looking for the sort of light that will enhance the features of your garden and create mystery and atmosphere.

Remember, you are not trying to imitate the sun – a vain hope at best – and rather than having a few, bright lights, it is usually far more effective to provide rather more lights of lower output, so that you can introduce texture and pattern and interest. The number and power of these will depend on the size of your garden, on how you want to use it, on the sections of it you want to light and on the amount of money you want to spend.

Contrast

The quality of light is defined as much by its absence as its presence. It is the balance between these two extremes that we will be using in the garden, the contrast between light and shade. This balance between light and dark, as expressed by contrast, is something that should be well known to anyone who watches television – too much light and everything washes out, too much dark and you cannot see a thing. Contrary to what many people believe, it is shadow that gives shape and form to an object, not light. By using the contrast between the lit and the unlit, we can bring out the shape of objects, change the shape of individual features and even create the illusion of objects that are not actually there.

It is rarely altogether dark at night. If the weather is good enough for you to want to be outside, there is usually some light from the moon or stars, and if you are in an urban environment, there is always some level of ambient light. This ambient light, however, which is borrowed from sources outside the garden, is, by definition, unfocused and is usually a general, bland, wash. The whole intention of introducing lighting outdoors is to create illuminated focal points that look dramatic precisely because they are in direct contrast with an area of darkness.

Despite the local ambient light level, most of us will have plenty of opportunity to exploit areas of light and darkness in the garden. Unless you are unfortunate and have a street light overhanging your garden, the night is usually dark enough to provide deep shadows, and it is these that we will exploit to give form and shape to the features we want to light, and to give us more than just illumination.

AVOIDING GLARE
Because the level of ambient light in a garden is usually lower than indoors, it is especially important to place luminaires carefully to avoid glare.

A narrow flood, placed bottom left, illuminates the trellis, throwing patterns of shadow from the plants, while the small spot downlighter to the right provides support accent.

Angle and Direction

The balance between light and shade brings out the shape of a object, giving it its three-dimensional form. This is known as modelling, but it is not achieved just through the creation of contrast. As significant as contrast in the modelling of trees, shrubs, architectural detail, statuary and so on are angle and direction. We are all probably aware of this phenomenon, without, perhaps, thinking about its causes. Those of us who live north or south of the tropics will see angle and direction at work every day in the early morning and late afternoon. The long shadows that are cast by the rising and setting sun will show up the contours and subtle details of a piece of ground, even one that can look quite flat at noon. This is an effect that is familiar to

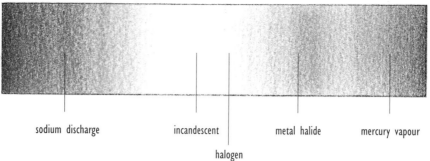

sodium discharge   incandescent   metal halide   mercury vapour

halogen

Different types of lamp produce light
with a different colour temperature.

archaeologists, who are often able to identify long-lost sites under these circumstances. Minute variations in a surface will frequently show up only when the light falls on it at an oblique angle. In the same way, artificial light, shone at a similarly shallow angle, will pick up surface texture and architectural details in buildings and can be used to bring out the shape and form of trees and shrubs.

Often, you will achieve a better result with two light sources, one to establish an object's outline and the other to give it mass. A light placed behind and slightly to one side of a dense shrub, for example, will define its shape; another placed in front of it and also slightly to one side, will define its form. This principle, of course, applies to many objects in the garden, including statues, and it is fundamental to designing the lighting of any three-dimensional object.

Colour

Colour is complex, and it is important to understand that we are dealing with two things, light and pigment. In the remainder of this section we will be looking at light. Pigment is discussed under Coloured Lamps and Filters (see page 41).

All colour is produced by the absorption or reflection of the various wavelengths that go to make up white light. White light, or visible light, is made up of the six wavelengths of red, orange, yellow, green, blue and violet. If the light is made up of fewer than the full set it has a different effect. Light that is made of only one wavelength is known as fully saturated, and the more saturated the light, the weirder the result. An example of a highly saturated light with which we are all familiar is that produced by sodium vapour lamps, the street lighting that is so common on major roads throughout the world. You only have to think how a red car turns brown under this sort of street lighting to realize that the wrong choice could be disastrous. Fortunately, most artificial light sources are designed so that they are as close to white as possible, so that the colours around us appear 'normal'.

Different types of lamp produce different qualities of light. Each type of lamp will produce light with a different colour temperature – that is, a different wavelength or position in the spectrum. The colour temperature of light is measured in degrees Kelvin. What we call white light has a temperature of between 3500 and 4500°K. The higher the temperature, the bluer the light; the lower the temperature, the redder the light. The spectrum ranges from ultra-violet down to infra-red, but most lamps are designed to be as close to the centre of the spectrum as possible so that they give good colour rendering and a middling warm light. Some lamps, however, have been developed largely for efficiency but, as a by-product, can produce interesting effects. These are the high-pressure discharge lamps, which tend to have colour temperatures towards the extremes of the visible spectrum.

What is significant about the high-pressure lamps is their relatively poor colour discrimination compared to incandescent or halogen lamps, which means that they will cause things to appear to change colour. Sodium is probably the worst offender, but the others also suffer from the problem to some extent. Although I have called this a 'problem', it need not be one, for like many other apparent limitations, it can be turned to our advantage. If we know what a lamp will do, which colours it will enhance and which it will limit, we can choose them quite deliberately. Sodium will enhance reds and yellows but will wash out the blue end of the spectrum, turning everything a strange, somewhat lurid, orange. At the other end of the scale, mercury vapour will do precisely the opposite. This characteristic is useful to us because it results in a cold, blue light that is similar to moonlight, and we can use this to good effect.

All the discharge lamps, whether they are low pressure, such as domestic fluorescent lamps, or high pressure, such as mercury vapour lamps, were developed with efficiency in mind – for example, a 11W fluorescent lamp will produce the same amount of light as a 60W incandescent lamp. They were not intended to do away with incandescent lamps in all circumstances, however, but only in those situations where their relatively poor colour discrimination is of no consequence. We can use these lamps deliberately, but you should be sure that you understand precisely the effect your choice will have, because it will be expensive if you get it wrong. Ironically, lamp manufacturers are constantly developing new ways of overcoming the colour discrimination problems, and the visual differences are becoming increasingly subtle.

One last word about the high-pressure lamps: they are nearly all physically large, and the fittings designed to carry them are correspondingly big. Unless you have a large garden or need to illuminate something very tall, you probably won't want to use them in your garden anyway.

Intensity

Intensity is the key to contrast and, therefore, to modelling. Where you position the light source is important, but the wrong balance of intensity could ruin the effect you are trying to achieve, no matter how well placed and focused the lights are.

Intensity – that is, the brightness of light – is measured in lumens, and it is determined by three factors: the wattage of the lamp, the width of the beam, and the distance the light source is from the object it is

Colour temperature

The majority of domestic lamps are similar in colour temperature, although lamps with different wavelengths have different colours – long-wave light, for example looks red, while short-wave light looks blue. Do not confuse colour with pigment (see page 41).

Reds and yellows

High-pressure sodium – the ubiquitous motorway lamp (2100°K)

Incandescent – most ordinary domestic lamps (2700°K)

Whites

Quartz halogen – the common lamp for low voltage (3100–5000°K)

Greens and blues

Metal halide – often used in urban streets (4000–6000°K)
Mercury vapour – often used in urban streets (4200–5900°K)

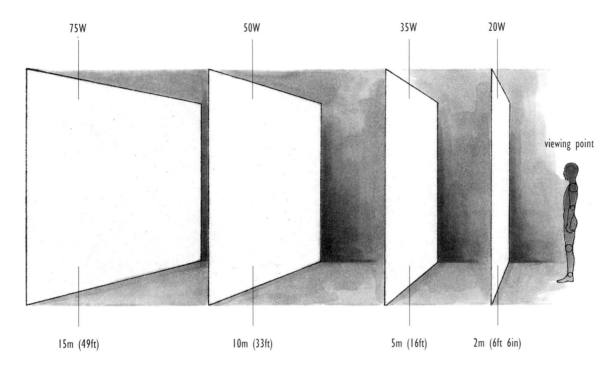

75W   50W   35W   20W

viewing point

15m (49ft)   10m (33ft)   5m (16ft)   2m (6ft 6in)

An example of good wattage balance
for halogen lamps.

lighting. The size of your garden or the part of it that you are illuminating will have to be taken into account in this – clearly you won't want something the equivalent of a searchlight in a small town garden. Intensity is not how much light generally, but how much light specifically, in direct relation to the subject, is provided.

Wattage

When you consider the intensity of light, probably the first thing you think about is the wattage. The more watts, you might think, the brighter the light. This is not necessarily true, however, and two factors will make a difference.

The first of these factors is focus. It is a curious phenomenon that if you take two lamps of the same wattage, one with clear glass and one with frosted (or pearl) glass, the frosted one will appear to be brighter. Similarly, if you have a projector of the same

wattage as an all-round-glow lamp, the projector will appear brighter, since it is focused only in one direction.

The second factor affecting intensity is the difference in the light output of different types of lamp. Tungsten filament lamps – the ones we are familiar with in the home – are usually between 40W and 100W, and we will all have a fairly good idea of what that means in terms of brightness. Halogen lamps, however, produce much more light at lower wattages – they are usually between 20W and 75W for a similar range of light output. A 70W metal halide lamp, an 80W mercury vapour lamp and a 100W quartz halogen lamp will all produce a similar lux output.

Low- and high-pressure discharge lamps are different again. An 11W fluorescent lamp will produce as much light as a 60W tungsten filament lamp, for example.

Beam Width and Distance

Intensity is also affected by the width of the beam and how far it is away from the subject.

Beam width is important for bringing out the modelling of specific objects. A broad width gives good general light, whereas a narrow beam will throw in highlights and sparkle. But the beam width is also significant when it comes to deciding how bright a beam you want. A very wide angle beam will throw less light on to an object than a narrow one set at the same distance, so you will need to position your luminaires relative to the lamps you mean to use. If, for example, two luminaires are set at the same distance from the subject, one wide and the other narrow, the wide one will need a brighter lamp if you want the two beams to be equally intense.

You could alter the brightness of the luminaire relative to the subject by moving it. If you do so, however, you will alter the width of the beam – the closer it is, the narrower it will be and vice versa – and if the width is important to the effect you want, you will have to use a different lamp.

Depth of Field

The importance of the depth of field may not be immediately obvious, but it is an aspect of lighting your garden that requires careful consideration. If you have a large depth of field – that is, if you are lighting objects that are close to you as well as objects that are far away – you will need to balance the brightness of the luminaires so that you do not get a distorted view. Lights that are close to the viewer will need to have relatively low output – that is, a lower wattage – so that they do not overpower those at a distance.

You should chose wattages that will let you achieve a balance across the whole lighting scheme, so that the effect you have planned will actually work. As a rough guide, divide your garden into foreground, middle ground and background relative

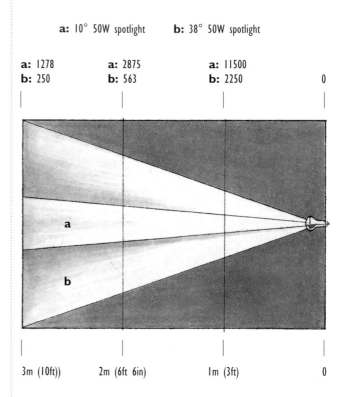

a: 10° 50W spotlight   **b:** 38° 50W spotlight

| **a:** 1278 | **a:** 2875 | **a:** 11500 | |
| **b:** 250 | **b:** 563 | **b:** 2250 | 0 |

| 3m (10ft)) | 2m (6ft 6in) | 1m (3ft) | 0 |

The intensity of light depends on wattage but also on beam width and the distance between the light source of the object. The output (measured in lux) of two 50W spotlights, one with a beam width of 10° and the other with a beam width of 38°, will vary considerably.

to the viewing point. The foreground can be anything within 3m (10ft), the middle ground 3–9m (10–30ft) and the background anything over 9m (30ft). If you are using halogen lamps on a 12V system, keep all the lights in the foreground between 20 and 35W, the middle ground 50W and those further away 70W or more.

You should remember that you may have more than one viewing point and that some of the lights will, therefore, be seen from at least two places. Using the depth of field in this way will make sure that you end up with a lighting scheme that does not cancel itself out and in which one light is not eclipsed by another.

Analysing Illumination

It is said that there are only three conjuring tricks in
the world and that every other trick is a variation on
one of these three. I suspect this is true of a great
many specialisms, and lighting design is no exception.
Whether you are working indoors or out, you will be
using a relatively small number of well-defined
techniques, and in the garden nearly all the lighting
will be done by using only one or two of them.

When you are planning a lighting scheme for
outdoors, there are two main differences from
lighting for indoors. One is obvious – there is no
ceiling; the other is that the scheme will be largely
composed of accent light.

Because there is no ceiling in your garden, the
lighting will be mostly uplighters in some form, as
opposed to interior domestic lighting, which uses
relatively little uplighting. Another important
difference is that outside we are, more often than
not, designing light to be looked at rather than light
to see by – not many people would choose to go
into the garden at night to read a book. The lighting
in the garden will be done for effect and as a
spectacle, and it will use, almost exclusively,
projectors of one sort or another. Otherwise,
however, there is not a great deal of difference
between the ways we use light outside and the ways
we do so inside.

Accent Light

Accent light is what garden lighting is really all about.
It is for lighting the specific rather than the general,
and it is the prime tool for modelling objects. Accent
lighting can be used on any scale, from intimate,
miniature spots in the near foreground to large power
spots for trees and tall buildings. A carefully placed
spotlight will bring out all the surface detail of an
object or will define its shape, especially if it is
three-dimensional – a statue, for example, or
something that has a highly textured surface.

Compact spotlights such as these are ideal for accent
lighting at the small end of the scale.

Groups of objects, accent lit, in careful balance
with, and in relation to, each other, is what most
good garden lighting schemes are made of, and the
effect is most often achieved by one of two means,
uplighting or downlighting. This is not surprising
since it is the only way of avoiding glare. Any light
set to shine on the side of an object is likely to get in
your eyes as you move around the garden, and it will
certainly annoy your neighbours. Glare is the enemy
of all lighting schemes.

Uplight

Uplighting is the most used tool in the repertoire, and it is probably the most useful. Illuminating the underside of objects, high or low, or throwing light up the side of a building or parts of a building produces some of the most dramatic effects possible. It is as exactly opposite to the way we perceive things in daylight as the day is to the night itself, giving us the additional advantage of allowing us to see things in a quite different way and firing our imaginations by showing us new aspects of what are, often, familiar objects.

Uplight is not necessarily or exclusively produced by luminaires designed for the purpose. It is, rather, an idea, which can be achieved with any projector or suitably shielded luminaire. However, designated uplighters, especially recessed uplighters – that is, those made to be buried in the ground – are particularly effective.

A common form of uplighter, seen in many exterior lighting schemes, is the power flood, which is usually built to carry a high-pressure discharge lamp, such as metal halide or mercury vapour, and which can give an enormously powerful light, often in a broad spread. Such uplighters are less often used in domestic schemes because they are so powerful.

Downlight

Downlighting is far less useful than uplighting. That is not to say that it is the least used method, however – far from it, alas. All too often you will see a single luminaire placed high on a wall, flooding the surrounding area with a soul-less and featureless light that achieves nothing except to irritate the neighbours and keep the birds awake all night.

That is not to denigrate downlight or deny its good uses. It is ideal for illuminating cooking and eating places, just as it would be in the kitchen or dining room. It can work well in pergolas and other semi-covered areas for picking out details such as a specimen shrub or a particularly interesting pot.

Remember, however, that if you use any kind of lighting in places like this it is important that the brightness is not so great that it eclipses the lighting in the rest of your garden. It is often a good idea to be able to turn it off or down independently of the rest of your lighting.

Downlight can also be used in garden structures, such as arbours or gazebos, where it is often the best form of lighting, especially if the structure is an old feature. It can also, if you are careful and have the right conditions, be used high up in a tree to simulate moonlight, and this can be extremely effective, although it should be used with caution, since it is not easy to integrate it within a larger scheme because it relies on a mild deception and because any other lighting around it will tend to give the game away. On the whole, downlighting should be used only when it is appropriate and, certainly, should be used with care.

Colour and Tone

One thing that it is important to bear in mind when you are using colour is that it is emphatically artificial and you should be careful with it. A green light shone on to a green surface such as grass will not make it look natural – quite the contrary, it will make it go green but, because of the limited colour range available, it will be an unnatural green. Coloured light can look impressive, but it is essentially light for its own sake, as opposed to illumination, and it should be used with that in mind. Reserve the use of colour for special effects, and then only if you know what you are doing.

As we have seen (page 36) different lamps have different colour discrimination, and you can use this characteristic to emphasize the colour of objects. Cool blue light will imitate the moon, warm yellow light will enhance the natural colour of plants and so on. It is possible to overstate this – the differences can be subtle, and if you want coloured light, you will be better off using coloured lamps or filters.

Coloured Lamps and Filters

It is unfortunate that coloured lamps come in a limited range of colours. I have no doubt that economies of scale have an influence on this, but the result is that it is possible only to get strong primary colours – red, blue, green, yellow is about it, although amber is available if you can find it. The most common are the standard tungsten filament lamps, used for party strings and so on, and coloured decorative GLS or PAR spots. Enclosed dichroic lamps are available with coloured glass, and halogen luminaires are often supplied with the means to insert a coloured glass filter, but, again, they are usually only available in a limited range.

The gels – that is, pieces of heatproof, coloured plastic – used in theatre and film lighting come in a wide range of colours, but I know of no luminaires outside the theatre that are made with the means to hold gels, and of a domestic scale, and you would probably have to invent your own. If you do, make sure you use the right materials – proper coloured gel is designed for the purpose and is inflammable. Never use flammable materials near a light source.

Startling effects can be achieved with coloured lamps or filters, but such strong colours may not always suit everyone's taste.

Special Effects

Because garden lighting is more to do with show and spectacle than with illumination for practical purposes, it would be illogical not to include some discussion about the kind of lighting that is designed exclusively for show and spectacle. Even if you do not wish to include this type of lighting as a feature in itself, you may be interested in the lighting that is more commonly seen in night-clubs and on stage in theatres or at concerts. Much of this will be beyond the scope of most garden projects, and there will be few people who will either want or, indeed, be able to afford to do it – this sort of thing can be expensive. In truth, it has less to do with lighting your garden than it has to do with decorative lighting in general, but a few ideas of this sort are worth mentioning.

The type of lighting I have in mind would be neon or luminaires fitted with motorized colour wheels, or 'gobos' with or without animation wheels, all of which are common in theatres and nightclubs. A colour wheel is what the name suggests: it is a wheel with discs of coloured gel or glass arranged in a circle. When it is turned by a motor, a beam of light shone through them will change colour. Colour wheels are used extensively in night-clubs and so forth as part of a of motorized light effects. Gobos are thin plates that have had a pattern cut out of them so that they throw the shadow of that pattern when you shine a projector through them and aim it at the wall or floor. The shape can be anything from a company logo to an abstract pattern, and you quite often see them in such places as show rooms. These patterns can be animated by fitting another wheel over the top, which is turned slowly by a motor. The combination of gobo and animation wheel produces an illusion of flames or rain or snow or leaves blowing in the wind, and it is often used in theatres.

Such lighting effects can be used in the garden, but they only really work when they have been done by a professional designer, who will have used them as part of an overall scheme. You may think they are irrelevant in a book about garden lighting because effects such as these are expensive and may well be beyond the average budget, but projecting moving light on to a rock or a tree can be a beautiful sight.

There are a number of effects, however, that are well within the reach of all. An inexpensive and relatively simple effect might be to string festoons of tiny lamps within a tree or among the planting along the side of a path. It is increasingly common to see 'Christmas tree' lights used outside at various times of year, and the products available are becoming more interesting and easier to find. You must make sure that the lights you get are intended for exterior use, or you might well find yourself in difficulties.

FIBRE OPTICS

Fibre optics is the term applied to those luminaires that project light down a filament or, more commonly, a bundle of filaments of optical glass or plastic. Luminaires using loose bunches of single filaments have been around for a long time as decorative features for the home. They have no practical application, being purely ornamental but, as such, they are fine.

A more serious application for fibre optics is in the realms of museum-type displays, because they can produce light that is almost totally non-destructive. A number of filaments, often hundreds of them, are bundled together and sheathed to make what are known as tails. These tails are fitted to a light source, and the light is carried down the tails to a focusing lens on the other end. Depending on the power of the light source, a surprisingly strong light is produced, even when the tail is several feet long.

Fibre optics are extremely useful for getting a good deal of light into small, awkward places. They would be excellent, for example, for lighting a small waterfall. The major drawback is cost; fibre optic lighting is frighteningly expensive and only the most exceptional circumstances are likely to be able to justify its use.

The tiny accent glow given by this candle lantern will be quite bright enough to illuminate its subject and bring a small corner to life.

Non-electric Lighting

So far we have talked exclusively about electric light, but it is far from being the only form of effective light for gardens. Because exterior lighting is mostly light to be looked at and to provide only sufficient light to get around, it does not have to be bright. Its prime purpose is to provide interest. Candles, flares and oil lanterns are possible alternatives, and the beauty of

flame is the movement it brings. A candle flickering in the dark has a unique quality, which is unparalleled when it comes to expressing romance and mystery. You do not have to restrict yourself to the lanterns you find on sale; it is easy to make a suitable lantern from a variety of found objects. As long as it is non-combustible, even a humble flowerpot can be used to make a candle lantern.

Many garden centres sell flares and special candles, which can look magical, and there are some attractive candle lanterns available. They may be harder to find than the candles themselves, but there are several companies importing stone lanterns from China and Japan or manufacturing reproduction ones. Companies that make garden ornaments are likely to offer lanterns of some sort.

Oil lamps are less common, but they are portable and there is nothing to stop you taking an indoor oil lantern with you when you go out into the garden. They provide a particularly good light for eating by.

Non-electric lighting is ideal for parties and special occasions. Oil lamps and candles are not cost-efficient, nor will they give out much light, of course, but then they are not meant to. However, do not ignore these alternative forms of light, if only because they can be fun and interesting. They introduce movement and, like fire itself, are attractive just as objects in themselves.

A modern design based on an ancient idea – a small oil lamp with a carved stone body. Not really meant to be practical, these are very attractive when used in groups or strings to light a path or terrace.

Not only interesting but beautiful, the traditional Japanese candle lantern gives light, focus and quiet elegance.

Seeking professional help

Amateurs should not contemplate installing an exterior electrical scheme, no matter how confident they feel about their skills. Using a professional electrical contractor is essential, but it can be difficult to know if your design is practicable and could be installed successfully, and it may help you feel confident about choosing an electrician if you have some idea about the aspects of the job that will affect the timing and cost. Below is a checklist of the questions you should ask an electrician who is quoting to do the job for you. They are in no particular order.

- *Is my domestic power rating sufficient for my proposed lighting scheme?*

- *Might I need a secondary consumer unit?*

- *I have small children and dogs. What steps should I take to ensure their safety?*

- *I want to include a pump for a waterfall and power in my outside workshop. Will single-phase power be sufficient or will I need to upgrade to a three-phase system?*

- *I want to divide the installation into more than one circuit. Will that complicate the wiring to a great extent? If so, is there a way of modifying the scheme without having to compromise the results I want?*

- *I would like to switch the lights on and off from several different places. Will that require complicated wiring? If so, is there a way of modifying the scheme without having to compromise the results I want?*

- *I would like to be able to switch sub-groups of lights on and off both locally and from the house. Will that require complicated wiring? If so, is there a way of modifying the scheme?*

- *Is the total light output too strong or too weak for the situation? If so, how can the scheme be adapted appropriately and cost-effectively?*

- *Can we establish the best routes for the cabling that will cause the minimum damage to the garden while remaining cost-effective?*

- *Will the electrician be responsible for ordering all the materials and equipment?*

- *Will the electrician provide the labour?*

- *Will the electrician provide a plan of the final installation that shows the routes of all the cables and locations of all the fittings, transformers and so on for future reference? (Providing such a plan will also be useful for you to note down the wattages of the lamps you finally decide to use for the garden, so that anyone can carry out future re-lamping without spoiling your design.)*

- *Finally – and you should never forget to ask – how long will the project take to complete?*

PLANNING
your
LIGHTING

When you are thinking about introducing lighting to your garden, you must bear in mind two facts: first, it may well cost a good deal of money, and second, it will be difficult to change once it is done. In your home, if you don't like a light you have put in, it will often be a simple matter of unplugging it and plugging in another. Outdoors, it is a different matter. It is unlikely that there will be a ready-made power circuit, and, even if there is, you will be unable to plug into it, as you can in the house. The luminaires will have to be hard-wired into the system and the cables buried in the ground in conduits, and it will not be an easy job to change anything. Exterior light fittings can be expensive, particularly if you have a large garden with, for example, very tall trees. In order to light these properly you are going to need comparatively powerful lights, which are not cheap. It is, therefore, essential that you know just how much light you really want or need and where you want it before any work is undertaken.

It doesn't matter what shape your garden is nor how small – even a windowbox can benefit from attractive lighting – the really important questions to consider are what sort of garden you have and what you use it for.

The garden as part of the house. The
lighting here is a combination of
sources both inside and outside the
house, planned so that the distinction
between the two becomes blurred.

Analysing Your Garden

Broadly, there are two types of garden: those that you can see the whole of from one place, and those that divide into 'sub-gardens', discrete areas that are not visible from any single point. No matter how extensive or how many exotic features may be included, all gardens fall into one of these categories.

Deciding how you use it can be done almost as easily. You should ask yourself: 'Do I want to sit in the house and look out at my garden?' 'Do I want to be able to walk around it at night and, if so, are there other places where I might want to sit and look at the garden?' Try to invent your own questions – from your answers you can begin to construct your ideas.

It is not just the big trees and imposing views that merit attention, for lighting the details is as important as any other part of an outdoor scheme.

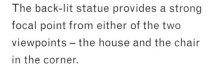

The back-lit statue provides a strong focal point from either of the two viewpoints – the house and the chair in the corner.

Viewpoints

Many larger gardens have more than one place that is considered to have a good 'view' – that is, some feature within the garden or, perhaps, a distant feature within the surrounding landscape that has been deliberately included in the garden design. Many of these viewpoints will be a bench or garden seat placed under a tree or beside a small lawn. One viewpoint may have more than one view, one at a distance (perhaps panoramic) and another being a close-up detail. Some may be more complicated, involving paving and a table for example, and some may be covered with a roof of some sort. An arbour or some other form of garden structure, such as a gazebo, would make a good viewpoint if there was something you could sit on, and you might want to install some lighting inside the structure as well as outside it.

Wherever you choose to sit and look, the object at which you look should have a carefully considered structure, with at least one clearly defined focal point or one main point with a second or even a third subsidiary one. This is true of garden design in general, but it is particularly so of garden lighting. Simply installing lights in a careless way may result in conflict, end up looking a mess and prove to be an expensive mistake. Deciding on the number of places in which you might want to sit will determine the extent of the lighting you will need to install, and this will determine how extensive the wiring will have to be, of what rating and how much the installation is likely to cost.

Set Pieces

Unless you intend just to flood your garden with light or are only putting in enough to reach the shed, the set pieces, in combination with their viewing points, are what makes the 'design' of your garden lighting. By set pieces I mean groups of lights that are designed to illuminate a specific object or group of objects, whether they be plants or manmade things – a statue on a plinth, set in a discrete position and backed and balanced with well-placed shrubs, for example. The set piece, therefore, could be anything that you decide is going to be the focal point of your viewing place. It is also possible that the lighting itself may be the set piece, providing its own focal point without the need for any specific object or group.

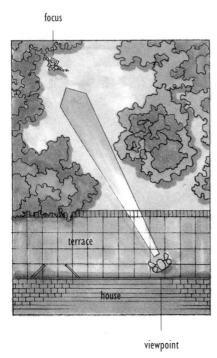

A single viewpoint and view.

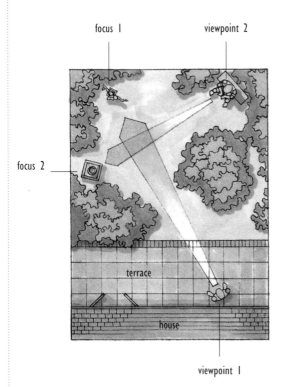

Multiple viewpoints and views.

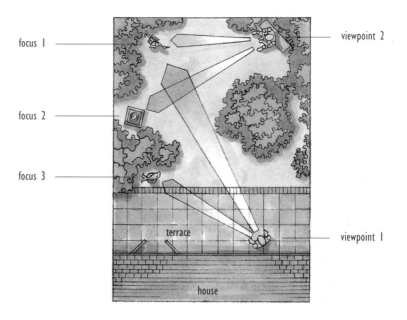

Multiple viewpoints and views.

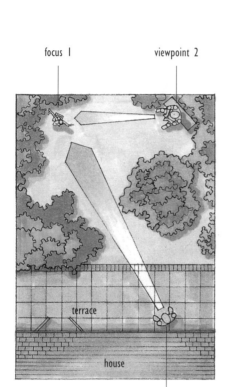

Multiple viewpoints but a single view.

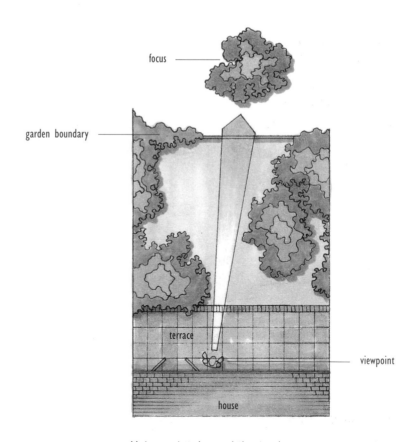

Using a view beyond the garden.

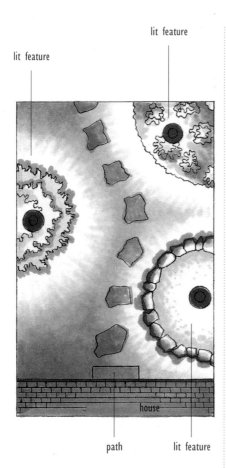

lit feature

lit feature

lit feature

house

path   lit feature

A path lit by overspill from other lit features.

A perfect set-piece for a small garden or an intimate corner within a larger area. The eye is drawn up towards the focal point of the figure, and this is reinforced by the light.

Route Illumination

If there are enough set pieces within the overall garden you may have all the light you want from the overspill from their lighting. In a larger garden, however, the set pieces may be so far apart that you need to illuminate the spaces between so that you and, more importantly perhaps, your visitors can get around the garden without hazard. On the other hand, route lighting may be all you need to provide a pleasant walk without the need to stop anywhere. Remember, if you want to light paths separately from the set pieces, your wiring will become more complex, with all which that implies in planning and expense.

Power Levels

This is when you should seek the advice of a qualified electrician. It is no use planning an extensive lighting scheme if you do not have enough power to run it. Larger gardens, particularly if they have powered water features, may well need three-phase power – that is, a system that is designed to supply three separate alternating currents of the same voltage at the same time – and few domestic homes will have this already in place. It is possible you will want to run mains power to secondary distribution points around the garden to facilitate local switching or from which you can run secondary low-voltage systems. Whatever your needs and plans, early decisions about power consumption are unavoidable. Always consult a professional.

Mains or Low Voltage?

Lights with a high output tend to be mains voltage; those with lower output tend to be low voltage, often 12V or 24V. Choosing between mains and low voltage or, indeed, having a mixture of the two, can be difficult. Your decision will largely depend on the scale of the things you are lighting. By this, I do not just mean the size of your garden but the size of the objects or groups of objects within the garden. Small gardens might well be better off with a low-voltage system since the fittings will be correspondingly small. A medium-sized garden might be able to take the larger high-output fittings, but many gardens are not large enough to be able to cope with, never mind need, such things as high-pressure discharge lights or the more powerful luminaires of the type intended for lighting public buildings. Some larger gardens may well have mature trees set in wide open spaces where such a light level would be appropriate but others may have little open space and, instead, dense planting with discrete places that will need more subtle treatment.

A typical D-I-Y low-voltage set, inexpensive to buy and easy to install.

Small, low-voltage light fittings go well in an intimate setting even if that setting is part of an extensive garden.

Garden lighting products tend to fall into three distinct groups. At the bottom end of the scale are those intended for the type of tiny garden that is often found in towns and cities and in which there is often only room for the D-I-Y kits that can be bought from garden centres. These are usually low voltage systems and are intended to stand alone, running off a single transformer plugged into a socket inside the house or immediately outside it.

Such systems will require no permanent wiring because they are designed to be surface laid and connected at random. They clearly present few problems; your main concern may be how to hide the wires without the possibility of losing them. This sort of lighting does have one major drawback, however: because few manufacturers have ventured into this market, there is little choice, especially in the UK.

At the top end of the range are products designed for gardens on the grand scale and for public spaces, large-scale landscaping and architectural illumination.

Large gardens can take a mixture of low and mains voltage, depending on the scale of the features and how close the viewer might be, but the overall systems will be extensive enough to demand hard mains voltage wiring to subsidiary distribution points even if, from there on, the wiring is stepped-down low voltage.

Medium-sized projects are more of problem. These might use either low or mains voltage luminaires, or a combination of both, but both types will need to be hard-wired into a properly installed system.

To a large extent, of course, the decision will be dictated by the kind of effects you want to create and your choice of luminaires. Several companies now include at least some smaller scale exterior lighting fittings in their product ranges, and a local wholesaler or a high street retailer dealing in exterior lighting, of which there are not many, will be able to show you catalogues and guide you through the decision-making process.

THE SWITCHING ARRANGEMENTS WILL HAVE A DIRECT EFFECT ON THE COMPLEXITY OF THE WIRING

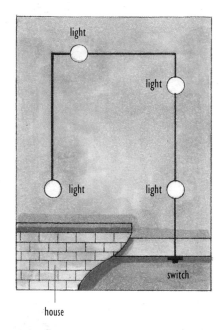
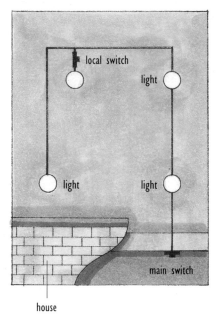
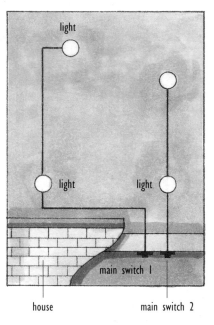

Simple wiring can be controlled from a single switch.

A light with a local switch will require separate wiring.

Two separate wiring systems may be required for a more complex layout.

Switching and Control

The complexity of the switching has a direct and fundamental effect on the wiring and, therefore, on the cost of the installation. The most straightforward way is simply to switch everything on and off from a point somewhere close to the distribution board. However, while avoiding all sorts of complications, this may not suit your ideas. You may, for example, decide that you would like to have a number of set pieces, viewed from points close to them, but that you don't want them all to be switched on all of the time, in which case you will want to be able to control them locally. If, at the same time, you want to be able to light the path that leads you to them, you will want to switch those lights from the house, particularly if it is a main approach to the house for visitors.

There are, in addition, possibilities for more sophisticated control than turning the light on and off. Just as indoors, automatic and programmable dimmer controls are possible in the garden; there is little limit to the level of automation should you wish it, but planning how you will control your lighting is every bit as important as planning the lighting itself and it must be done at the same time.

This bench has been made into a focal point by the lighting. Anyone sitting on it, however, might well wish to turn the lighting off while they are there, and local switching would therefore be imperative.

Take a chair around the garden so that you can establish your optimum viewing points, and design your lighting accordingly.

Drawing Up a Plan

The first step in planning anything is to get it down on paper. For gardening projects there is no need to be absolutely accurate, but you will want to know where everything really is – not just where you think it is – and, particularly where everything is in relation to where you want to look at it from.

Carrying Out a Survey

If you garden is medium sized or small, you could draw up a plan yourself. Measure and mark down the boundaries, features, paths and so forth on some squared paper, keeping everything to scale to avoid mistakes. It does not matter whether you use metrical or imperial measurement, just as long as you are consistent.

If you have a garden of 0.2 hectares (½ acre) or more it will be worth getting it properly surveyed by an architect or a surveyor. A survey of this sort need not be expensive, and once it has been drawn up, it will become an invaluable record of where everything is. It will tell you what you have above the ground, and, more importantly, it can be used as a record of what is below the ground – drains, soak-aways, electric cables, gas pipes and the like. Also, if

any old buildings have been demolished over the years, the plan can tell you where the old walls ran so that you can avoid them when you start digging the trenches for your lighting cables – or at least not be surprised by them. In years to come this type of survey will prove its worth over and over, not just for you but for any future owners or users of your garden.

Whether you draw up the plan yourself or have it prepared by a professional, for the purposes of planning your lighting it must show the position of the house, all the walls and fences, paths, steps and any other built objects. Mark all the established trees and shrubs, preferably including their canopy spread so that you will know at a glance where the best positions would be for the luminaires. It is also important to make a note of the spread of the canopy on your trees because the root system covers roughly the same area as the canopy, and your aim should be to disturb the roots as little as possible. Also mark the extent of your planting beds – you don't want to dig up the lawn unless you have to, and you may be able to get away with siting all the luminaires within areas of dug soil. Use the drawing to plan the best routes for your cabling and refer to it in the future to remember where you put them.

It may be thought that a detailed survey of this sort is more than anyone will need, and, if you are doing the design for yourself, it may be so. However, if you are going to ask a designer to help you with your scheme, you will save considerable time and expense by having a plan ready made.

What to Light

The aim of introducing light to the garden is not to try to recreate the sun by flooding the whole garden with light. Instead, you will have to decide what to light and from where you are going to be looking at the result. Some things will be obvious candidates: waterfalls and pools, specimen trees, groups of rocks with planting and so on.

It is often best to decide on your viewing points first. You may want to light an entire object so that you can wander around it, but it is more likely that you will be sitting somewhere specific, such as on a terrace or even looking out from inside a sitting room. So sit in these places and look at what you can see. Try to imagine being able to see only parts of the feature and to decide which parts would you want to see if you had to choose. Having chosen your scene, refer to the plan and mark roughly in pencil where you think lights should go. Then go round the garden, making sure that all the places so marked will actually work. Plan the best routes for any cabling and decide what sort of control system you are likely to want.

Choosing the Luminaires

You will probably have to go to wholesalers for the sort of luminaires you will need in the garden. Not many high street lighting shops will carry much in the way of outdoor fittings, beyond a few coach lamps and bulkheads. You will have to have a clear idea of what you want to buy before you go shopping, and this is another reason for consulting a designer or, at least, an electrician, who, if they are accustomed to installing exterior fittings, will know what type of luminaires will be suitable.

An early decision is whether you want to be able to see the luminaires or not. If you do not, you will probably want recessed fittings. If it doesn't matter or if the luminaire will be masked by something – a shrub or wall, for example – surface fittings will do. Surface fittings are a lot less fuss to install, and so they may be your first choice. Nevertheless, there are places where buried luminaires are necessary, such as in a driveway, where you can drive over them, or in a lawn, so that you can mow the grass easily.

An example of the more traditional style of outdoor lighting; this is for general illumination giving an all-round glow. Accent lighting would require projectors, however, so your choices are determined by both your need and the style of your garden.

Don't forget the scale of your garden. Many exterior luminaires are quite large objects in themselves, so, if you have a more intimate setting, you will want to seek out smaller, more discreet, fittings. These are likely to be low-voltage, using compact halogen lamps, so that decision may be made for you at the same time.

Using Your Imagination

Remember that introducing lighting to your garden is supposed to be fun. It is all too easy to get bogged down in the details and practicalities, but try to let your imagination run free. Keep a look out for inspiration whenever you are out and about, noting what other people have done, not just in private gardens, but also in restaurants, parks and public places, hotels and corporate buildings. Many public buildings are very well lit. I have often seen examples where the designer has mixed sodium and metal-halide lamps to achieve a contrast in colour that can look spectacular.

Business parks often include landscaped areas, many with lit features, and just because they are on a grand scale does not mean that you cannot find inspiration there. The same is true, perhaps more so, of theme parks. I am not suggesting that you should try to emulate the main set pieces, but the incidental lighting, perhaps of secondary buildings or odd corners, might suggest ideas for your own garden.

Look to nature for inspiration, too. Note how the sun shines through the trees and hedges, making delicate moving patterns, or how it throws long fingers of light and shadow across the fields early in the morning. The colour of sunlight varies throughout the day as well as in different weather. You may be able to incorporate some of these ideas into your design, but, more importantly, looking at nature helps you to understand what light actually does – how it influences the view and our feelings about it. Look at all these things, natural and manmade, for ideas and don't be afraid to imitate.

This tranquil scene may not reflect the level of frustration and delay that can occur in a garden lighting project, but the result will be well worth the effort.

Getting in the Experts

Now is the time to call in an electrical contractor. Make sure you do. Shop around until you find a contractor with specific experience of lighting in the landscape. A qualified person will be able to tell you straight away if your plan will work and help you to modify it if it won't, before you start spending money. They will know what size of cable you will need and where best to run it. They will also be able to tell you about wiring for complicated switching, centralizing transformers, voltage drop and so on and, most importantly, they will be able to make everything safe.

You will have to find someone to dig the holes and trenches. Your contractor should be able to help here, and you should discuss it with them anyway, for the sake of better coordination, even if you intend to find your own labour,

When the electrician lays in the wiring, make sure they leave at least 1 metre (1 yard) of free cable at the final connection point for each luminaire. No matter how careful you have been in positioning the lights on your plan, when it comes to fixing them in place you may well want to make some fine adjustments. Having a good length of free cable will enable you get the light exactly where you want it. For recessed luminaires dig a larger hole than you need and then back fill. The cable can be trimmed back as required. And have some spare lamps, too, just in case you want to change the wattage at the last moment.

Running the Project

Planning a scheme is the easy part. Getting it installed and up and running is another matter altogether, and it must be carefully controlled. Installation is not especially complicated, it is just that when things do go wrong, they can affect other stages in the process. Broadly, the timetable is:

- Source, select and order the luminaires you want.

- Order all other materials – cable, junctions, switches and so on.

- Dig the trenching for the wiring.

- Install the cable and back fill.

- If possible, temporarily connect the luminaires to carry out final positioning.

- Complete the installation and fully connect all the fittings, switches and so on.

- Check the final positions and change any if necessary.

A traditional coach lamp for general illumination.

Troubleshooting

Although everything should be straightforward, things can go wrong. It will, without doubt, be easiest to ask your contractor to order everything that will be needed. This will avoid numerous potential complications, not the least of which are breakdowns in communication. Be aware, too, of lead times. Many manufacturers hold only limited stocks and tend to make to order. Sometimes the luminaire you want will be made be a subsidiary in another country altogether, and you may find yourself waiting for up to 10 weeks, even months.

The time of year may be significant, particularly if you are faced with a long lead time and you started planning late in the year. If there is a prolonged spell of wet weather, the digging will, inevitably, be delayed, and if the delivery of any of the parts is held up as well, the timing for the project could be thrown completely awry, leaving you facing winter and no work started. At this point it might be better to wait until spring and better weather before starting again.

This is, of course, the worst possible case, but it could happen. It will only be a problem, however, if you haven't taken the possibility of it into account.

PLANS
and IDEAS

In this section we are going to look at some plans and ideas that you can adopt and adapt to suit your own garden. Some of these are drawn from schemes that I have done myself, and some are things I have seen others do. Every garden has different problems and challenges and each will present different opportunities. Gardens are as individual as their owners. As a consequence, many of the ideas may not fit directly into your own garden and will have to be modified. I have not tried them all myself – some are waiting for the right garden to come along so that I can try them out.

The easiest way discussing these ideas is to go at it piecemeal, so I have broken the garden down into its constituent parts. This is a useful exercise and one that you should go through yourself, since it will help you to understand what you are dealing with, but you should be careful not to lose sight of the idea of your garden as an entity. Every time you add lighting to one part of it, it will affect another part, and, if it is not to look a mess, it is important always to regard your garden as a harmonious whole. Always remember that a light placed to do a specific job in one place may be visible from another part or spill into another part of the garden where it may not be wanted. Even as you deal with each element separately, you should keep your mind's eye on the overall scheme so that your plan will bring all the elements together, and none will overpower another.

GARDEN FEATURES

Views, Viewpoints and Orientation

In much the same way that you would start designing a lighting scheme for indoors by listing activities and tasks, a good start outdoors is to analyse the garden and establish what you want to light. You will also need to decide how you are going to use your garden, and you should keep that use in mind when you select the objects you want to light. Every garden has one or more of a number of standard elements, and for the purposes of designing a lighting scheme, no matter how large or small, simple or complex the garden, it is useful to identify these elements and determine how they fit together.

Nearly everything within the garden will fall into one of three main categories: things to look at; places to look at them from; and routes to and from those places. For convenience, we will call these views, viewpoints and orientation. These are not mutually exclusive, of course – a viewpoint can easily be part of a view seen from a different part of the garden, for example. Some, perhaps many, will fall into more than one category, but there are differences that make it worth treating the groups separately. I also find it helps to make planning more straightforward if you know what each element will contribute to the overall scheme.

With the right lighting, it is possible to alter, visually, the whole scale of the garden. Indeed, the entire layout of the garden can appear to be altered by the careful use of light, and your perception of the garden and your understanding of its shape can, and often will, will be changed when you turn on the lights. It is even possible to invent features – it is not necessary for there to be a real path or steps, for example – lighting can create the illusion of their presence. Placing a series of small recessed lights or path-lighters across an otherwise pathless space, such as a lawn, can create the impression of a path. This

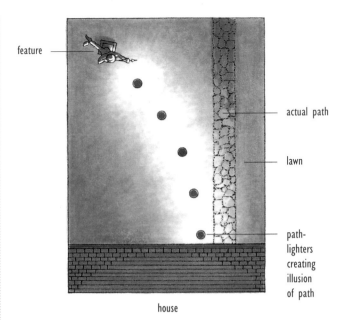

feature — actual path — lawn — path-lighters creating illusion of path — house

Lights can be used to create the illusion of, say, a path where none actually exists in order to draw attention to a feature.

technique enables you to focus a view by drawing the eye to a point of your choice – perhaps a statue or a specimen shrub. This may be a bit ambitious for the beginner, however, and so that you can get your teeth into the subject as quickly as possible we will start with how to light real things.

Remember, however, that it is every bit as easy to put too much light into a garden as into a house and with the same result of destroying the atmosphere. Think in advance of the type of atmosphere you want to create and don't lose sight of it among all the detail. Keep your mind on your overall plan.

Views

Views are, obviously, those things at which we look, but the term includes a huge range of objects – anything from an entire landscape to a single flowerpot. In many smaller gardens, the 'view' could easily be the whole thing, although you may feel it more appropriate to go for one or two carefully selected details within it. Large gardens will certainly need to be considered as a collection of details, and if it is not to look like a sports stadium, you will have to be selective about what you choose to illuminate. If you have a garden from which you can see out, remember to include the surrounding landscape in you lighting scheme, or, at least, don't ignore it. By dovetailing the lighting within your garden with light sources beyond its boundaries, you can extend those perceived boundaries into the far distance, on much the same principal as the designers of Japanese gardens may use the landscape without to focus and frame the landscape within. Take into account any light that is beyond your control so that it doesn't ruin what you want to do. It would be a great pity if you planned a delicate and intimate lighting scheme for a courtyard garden that was washed out by a street light outside.

Trees and Shrubs

The shape of a formal garden is established by the shapes of the beds, the borders, the pathways between them and the means employed to divide up the overall space, which could be hedges, fences or walls. Formal gardens often have small shrubs in beds or herbaceous borders that have been planted with carefully chosen colour groups and so on. In an informal garden, it is the trees and shrubs themselves that define the garden's shape and form.

Formal or informal, the shapes created by walls, trees, shrubs and so on during the day can be reinforced at night, the difference being that their shape and form will be defined by darkness rather than by light – that is, by the shadows they cast or are cast on to them. Each situation will be different, and the types of shrubs and trees you have will effect the way you light them, as will the formality or informality of the design.

If your garden consists of beds of small shrubs or mixed plantings of annuals and herbaceous plants,

The decision to light this group of pots would have been made as part of an overall plan. Without careful planning you would not know the effect this might have on the other garden lighting.

but without one dominant specimen plant, a good solution is to dot small lights in and around the lighting to create pools of interest. With low planting, downlight may be best – use directional spotlights mounted on posts or adjacent walls, for example, and try grazing light across the surfaces to bring out the texture. If you have taller plants, you may prefer to treat them as if they were a hedge and try uplighting them from a path or from within the bed.

Exactly how and where you position your lights will depend on the style of garden you have. Take your cue from the design – a formal garden can have symmetrically placed lights, while an informal garden would be better served with a more random placing. Whichever approach you adopt, make sure that you do not end up with a hotchpotch of unrelated lighting. Try to visualize the finished scheme and make sure that the end result has some internal cohesion and that you have a scheme that creates an overall picture and not just a scattering of light.

The trees are strongly lit from two incandescent light sources, in this instance PAR lamps in simple spike-holders, enhancing their natural colour. By contrast, the rock group in the foreground borrows its light from a path-lighter fitted with a light source much nearer the blue end of the spectrum. As a result you get an interesting colour contrast and a powerful impact.

This little light, placed among soft foliage planting, is ideal in such an informal setting and lights both the trellis and the path through it.

This mysterious effect is just the sort of lighting which makes for interest and appeal. The concealed, incandescent light brings out the natural colours of the foliage in contrast to the surrounding dimness.

If you have a large garden or your planting scheme consists of a few well-placed large shrubs or specimen trees, you should treat each one individually, while making sure that each separate element contributes to an overall plan.

A dense shrub or tree – a conifer for example – will benefit from lighting that brings out its modelling – that is, its shape and bulk. A light placed behind and slightly to one side will establish its size and outline by producing a silhouette, and another placed in front but, again, to one side will bring out its shape and texture. In all cases, make sure that you position the light sources so that they are not directly visible from the viewpoint. You can, for example, conceal them behind smaller plants or use a dip in the ground. Surface-mounted lights would be most suitable, but it might be possible to use recessed uplighters, although you would want to use the kind that allows you to tilt the lamp. Feature shrubs and

Low planting side-lit to bring out all the colour and texture of the flowers.

LIGHTING TREES
A light placed behind a dense tree or shrub will throw it into silhouette, emphasizing its shape and size only. When it is lit from the front and below, the tree's form is evident but there is no indication of scale. When two uplighters are used, the shape and size of the tree are revealed.

trees are often planted within a grassed area, and in these conditions a recessed uplighter may be particularly useful since, with the right fitting, you can mow straight over the top. If you do decide to do modelling lighting along these lines, remember about the differences in light output between a spotlight and a floodlight and how that is also influenced by distance (see pages 19–20).

A shrub with more open foliage can be lit from directly below, which will have the effect of illuminating the plant as if from the inside. This is when recessed uplighters come into their own, not least because of their convenience during lawn mowing. It is often possible to light the inside of the tree in this way and to light the outer surface of the canopy from a distance as well – but get the balance right so that the one does not cancel out the other. This technique of lighting the inside and the outside works best for deciduous trees with an ample canopy. Use a fairly narrow beam – certainly not more than about 35° – to avoid too much light spill, although that will depend on the scale of the subject and how far away from it you can position the luminaires.

A large garden may well have some very tall trees, and these will require correspondingly powerful lights. To light the canopy of, for example, a Scots pine of 9m (30ft) or more, you will need at least one strong spotlight placed no less than 2m (about 6ft) from the trunk. If you want to light the trunk itself you will probably need a second spot, set slightly closer and focused accordingly. A luminaire fitted with an ellipse lens, which will light the trunk without undue spill, would be especially appropriate here, and to get a powerful enough beam, you will almost certainly have to use an incandescent lamp. A problem with discharge lamps is that they are all-round-glow lamps, which make good floodlights but which need special luminaires, fitted with reflectors and lenses, to focus the light into a spot beam. Such luminaires tend to be large objects in themselves and may not be suitable for an average-sized garden.

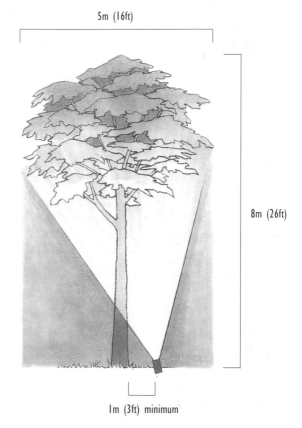

Positioning an uplighter beneath a tree.

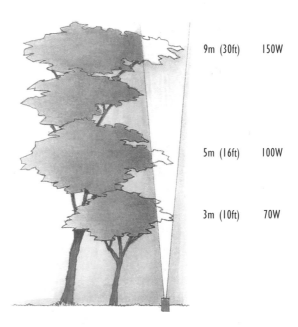

The wattage chosen will depend on the height required. This example is for a metal halide lamp.

light source   light source

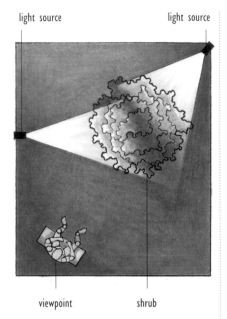

viewpoint   shrub

Position the light sources as
indicated to model a dense shrub.

directional uplighter   uplighter beneath tree

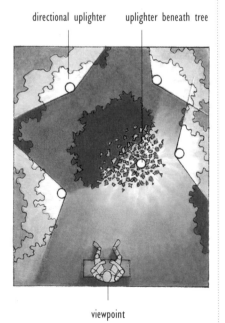

viewpoint

A tree in a clearing can be lit with
perimeter lighting.

In addition to defining a tree, light can also reveal the space the tree is in. If a small feature tree stands in a clearing among dense shrubs, putting a spotlight beneath it and placing recessed uplighters around the perimeter to illuminate the shrubs will reveal it and establish it in the context of its surroundings. A feature like this makes an attractive focal point when viewed from a distance, but if it is hidden within a larger garden, it can be truly mysterious and magical. When anything dramatic is revealed suddenly, it makes for interest and excitement, and this is one of the main pleasures of lighting in your garden.

And, of course, there is topiary. Much topiary would be well served by lighting. Whether it be formal abstract shapes or figurative representations of birds and animals it is all, in effect, sculpture. Just because it is not carved in marble does not mean it may not be lit. Often, however, the problem with topiary is its scale in relation to its surroundings. Many quite large examples are grown in rather restricted, crowded places, and getting enough distance to make sense of the shape can prove difficult. In circumstances such as these it is best to use your imagination and play with the shapes and juxtapositions rather than trying to illuminate the object. Of course, smaller pieces in open ground really do become sculptures and may be lit accordingly (see pages 72–5).

Above all, remember to keep the light for your trees and shrubs sympathetic. Try using different coloured lamps or gels to emphasize the natural colours of the tree or shrub. Light at the yellow end of the spectrum will bring out the greenness of deciduous foliage and grass in a way that green light will not; green light tends to make things appear sickly, which may be good for fun-fairs, but not so good for private gardens. Conversely, blue light can be a good choice for lighting coniferous trees, many of which have natural bluish tinge. For example, a mercury vapour lamp, which is at the blue end of the colour temperature scale (at anything up to 5900°K), and has relatively poor colour discrimination, would tend to emphasize the blue in the foliage. Having said that, however, unless you are confident and intend to use coloured light as a deliberate part of your design, it is better to stick to the middle of the spectrum, which means using incandescent lamps. Another good reason for staying with incandescent light is that the vapour lamps tend to be physically large, with big luminaires that may be out of scale with your garden.

Lawns

Lawns can be a problem, particularly if they are flat, level and neatly trimmed. Unless you want to provide light for a specific activity, direct light on to a lawn will produce little of any interest and, often, the light-spill from other features will be enough to give it, at least some, illumination. But look at nature and see what the sun can do with flat places. With a little imagination even a flat lawn can be transformed. If your lawn is of this flat and level style try using spots, or wide floods, with barn doors, which constrain the beams from spilling upwards. Aim them across the lawn from as near to the ground as possible, and preferably so that they shine through or past something else such as a shrub or a screen of some sort. This will project patterns of shadow across the lawn, thereby making a feature of the light itself. A really low light will pick up the texture of the grass, and any change of surface level, however slight, will also show up. This technique can be particularly successful where a lawn is partially concealed from view – a semi-hidden pool of light can give the illusion that the garden is larger than it really is and entice the viewer to explore.

If the lawn undulates or has sharp changes of level, or if the grass is kept long, as in a meadow lawn with, perhaps, a mown swathe forming an informal path, the possibilities become more interesting; what is possible is limited only by the imagination. Apart from the general warning about not floodlighting it as if it were a football pitch, there are no right or wrong ways, but do be careful with colour. Generally, low-level spot- or floodlighting is the best approach – the lower the better. Light shone down from a height will, inevitably, make your lawn resemble the sports field we are trying to avoid.

If you have a path across your lawn or next to it, some appropriate path-lighters will, in all probability,

provide all the light you need, at least to see by. But, for a more interesting result, if you have long grass, as in a meadow lawn, or if you can avoid mowing right up to the edge, try placing directional spotlights among the grass and plants to illuminate little patches, perhaps of specimen plants, such as wild herbs, or try scattering ground-level path-lights randomly in the grass to give a mysterious glow here and there.

A lawn within a formal garden might seem to present slightly more of a problem. It is quite possible that you will not want to spoil the formality with irregular shadows and you certainly won't want to let the grass grow overlong. A good approach is to use the formal structures within the garden to act as screens for the light sources so that you have brightly lit areas of lawn surrounded by the silhouettes of the retaining walls. Use lights fitted with barn doors or louvres, if possible, to constrain the light to exactly the shape of the grassed area. If you are more adventurous you might like to experiment with gobos with formal patterns, if you can find luminaires to carry them. Be prepared to do a little D-I-Y if you want to use accessories of this sort.

The lawn is one place where you can make a feature of the light source itself. You can use Japanese stone lanterns to good effect or an oil lamp of some sort. There is a good variety of lights, electric or otherwise, available from garden centres and specialist suppliers that are interesting in themselves as well as providing light to see by or, at least, enough to act as a guide around the garden. Many of the more interesting of those that are available for the domestic market do tend to be oil lamps and candles of one sort or another, and they might not be suitable for all situations, particularly if you want to be able to turn your lights on and off from inside the house.

Although man-made, this rocky waterfall has a natural feel. The two side-lights, placed low down, bring out all the solidity and strength of the rock, mostly through the shadows created by the low angle.

Rocks and Rock Faces

There can be very few of us who have large outcrops of natural rock in our gardens, but, for those of us who do, they present marvellous opportunities for lighting, the more so if they are combined with water. In some respects, rocks are like particularly dense shrubs and they can be lit in a similar fashion, by partially silhouetting them from behind with some modelling light falling on to the front surfaces. Free-standing rocks will often form part of a group, whether of more rocks or of complementary objects, such as plants, chosen for their shape. It is these shapes, singly and as groups, that give you the chance for some interesting lighting effects. Try putting small lights into the heart of a group of rocks to bring out their colour and form, with, perhaps, some side-light to place the group in context with the rest of the garden. Don't forget the potential of silhouette – a strong, interesting outline with a small tightly focused detail at the front would make a very dramatic set piece. Consider treating a free-standing rock or rock group as a piece of abstact sculpture.

Rocks can, however, be more than just three-dimensional objects. Because they are often relatively smooth, rocks provide good 'screens' for projecting on to, and, even on a small scale, bouncing light off water on to a rock produces fascinating moving patterns on its surface. Still patterns can be made by shining light through an open foliage plant on to the rock surface, in much the same way as one might do indoors through a potted plant on to the wall. This is enhanced all the more if the surface of the rock has an interesting texture or colour or, preferably, both.

Fences, Walls and Screens

You can treat fences, walls and screens in similar ways to rocks. Formal gardens are often laid out using walls and open fences to provide the underlying structure, and they are intended to be part of your view of the garden. This would be reason enough to consider lighting them, but, in fact, walls, fences and screens are often good things to light anyway. Fences, such as withy or hazel hurdles, have good surface texture and are excellent subjects for

The terrace is lit from the wall sconce but the light in the bed in front throws patterns on to the wall itself, bringing out its texture and colour and thereby making a feature of a necessity.

oblique lighting that is set to graze the surface and bring out the pattern of the structure. In fact, any low-relief surface can be lit in this way to good effect. But fences and open screens have another quality that can be exploited: they can be lit from behind so that the light is filtered and the construction is thrown into silhouette.

Back-lighting is a useful technique in many circumstances, but a wall that is built of glass bricks can be particularly well served by it. The glass is usually too thick to be transparent but it is excellent as back-projection screen. If you have a glass wall, try placing a spot to shine through a foliage plant and throw the shadows on to the back surface to create an interesting pattern – and movement when the wind blows.

Of course, in larger gardens, at least some of the screening might be done with plants and many gardens have hedges. If a hedge is closely clipped then it becomes, effectively, a green wall and presents a solid surface. But this surface has texture, particularly if it is not clipped too often or if it can be trained or clipped to have an uneven surface. There is a magnificent example of such a hedge at Montacute House in Somerset, England, which has been allowed to grow over the years into a fantastic abstract surface of lumps and bumps, many of which look almost as if they are strange figures or faces but none of which are. It is not lit as far as I know, but it would certainly make the most fabulous subject for lighting.

The foreground lighting of the pot group is all the more interesting because of what is happening behind it. The lighting to the open fence on the right provides a pleasing silhouette, and a concealed light brings out the texture of the wattle screen.

A tiny beam of light is here concentrated on the centre of this piece, making it appear to be lit from within. After dark the piece will look as if it is floating.

Statuary and Sculpture

If you ask if they have any sculpture in their garden, most people would be surprised and would almost certainly say no, but many more do have something of the sort than they would recognize. Statuary need not be grand: it could be as modest as a garden gnome, a bird bath or a sundial. Many garden centres sell mass-produced statuary of some description, and just because it is humble is no reason not to consider it a suitable subject for lighting.

There are those who would say that if you are going to the expense of installing lights, it had better be for a worthwhile subject. I would disagree with this view, because the intention is not just to illuminate it so that it may be examined but to make it work at night as it does during the day, irrespective of its merit as a piece of art. Whether or not you consider it to be 'art', it is worth thinking about how you might light it, particularly if it forms a centrepiece or a focal point. We are not necessarily talking about elaborate schemes; such an idea would work just as well for a modest figure as for a grand one. And, for our purposes, the question of the artistic merit of a piece is strictly irrelevant.

In general, the same rules apply for lighting statuary as for the shrubs and rocks, but there is one major difference: it is possible to distort the shape of something with light, which might not matter for a rock but which you might not want to do by accident if you are lighting a statue. With the right treatment though, lighting a piece of sculpture can add to its impact and even alter its perceived meaning. We have probably all, as children, played with electric torches, lighting our faces from strange angles to produce contorted masks, and it is exactly this technique that can be used to add impact to a sculpture at night, whether it is figurative or abstract. This must be done with caution, however, and it should be done deliberately. There is such a thing as a happy accident, but you would be unwise to rely on chance.

The artificial setting has been made to show off the light fitting, but the photograph demonstrates how even a relatively humble piece of sculpture can benefit from being lit. Incidentally, the light is positioned so that it throws interesting shadows on to the wall behind, thereby creating secondary interest.

Depending on the piece, light will help to define it and give it shape, but positioning, intensity and focus must be given particular attention. Again, low-level light set at an oblique angle is a good starting point, but experiment before deciding on the final position. If you are in the fortunate position of having a sculpture by a living artist, try to consult him or her about appropriate lighting – the artist may have strong feelings on the subject.

POSITIONING

The positioning and intensity of lighting will, of course, be determined largely by the sculpture itself, but much will also depend on what is adjacent to it. If it is standing alone, perhaps in a lawn, one option is to light it from luminaires mounted on to poles set at a convenient distance from the piece. This enables good control of the light sources and can be a good solution from a practical viewpoint, but it is not so good aesthetically. Ther is a reasonable selection of pole-mounted luminaires available but, since they are going to be visible, you will want to select them for their appearance and to suit the overall style of your

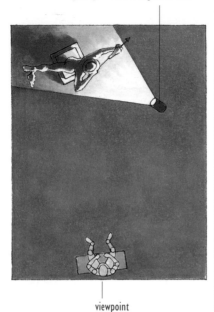

single light source at ground level

viewpoint

Positioning a light source in relation to a statue.

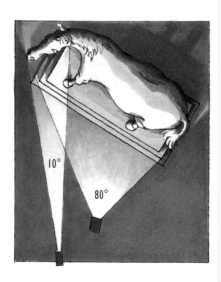

10°

80°

A combination of wide and narrow beams is suitable for a complex subject such as a statue.

garden. Tall pole-mounted lights may be intrusive during the day, in which case you may prefer to light your sculpture from ground level.

Almost certainly you will need more than one light – try a flood to one side and a spot to the other, or variations on this idea. If there is a conveniently sited tree or large shrub, you may be able to conceal small spots within it to pick up details, such as the face of a human figure. Side or top lighting will produce a quite different effect than lighting from below, and it is worth experimenting to find the perfect position. Try lighting it with a good torch, hand-held by a friend. This will enable you to see what effect different positions will have on the result.

INTENSITY

Apart from rendering it visible in the dark, the intensity and quality of the light you use to illuminate a sculpture should also be influenced by the materials used to make it. Soft sandstones, for example, have a red colour, whereas a stone such as Purbeck marble is close to white. All materials have their own intrinsic colour, which you should bear in mind when lighting them, and it may not be a question of a single material – stone and bronze are a fairly common combination, for example, and each material has its own different colour and texture.

Consider, too, the quality of the surface. Stone and wood are often left with a matte finish, but most can take a high polish and, along with the metals – steel and bronze, for example – can be polished and lacquered to give a highly reflective surface, which you must take into consideration. Avoid glare and flash – all you will see is the light, not the sculpture. If you imagine a mirror with many surfaces at different angles you can see the sort of problem you are dealing with. A number of small, relatively low-power light sources will produce sparkle, whereas a single, strong light is more likely to produce glare from at least one angle of view.

Where you place the light sources will have a bearing on this, too. Clearly, a spot placed at ground level and close to the piece will be less likely to produce reflections than one placed at eye-level.

FOCUS

Whether it is highly polished or not, because a sculpture will often have complicated surfaces, focus can have significant influence on the appearance of a piece. Again, a number of narrow spots, positioned to pick up details or to contrast areas of light and dark, may have much more impact than a single, bland, overall floodlight, no matter now effective that may be at the business of straightforward illumination. Focusing the light will introduce drama and add significantly to the

impact that a piece may have on the viewer.

Lighting sculpture is much more complex than lighting trees or shrubs. It is a problem that is not always well solved, so do not be afraid to experiment and remember that, while there are overall rules, each piece will benefit from individual consideration and, often, different treatment.

VIEWPOINTS

In a garden featuring a collection of sculptures the idea of distinct viewpoints is a slightly artificial one, for although you may well sit in certain spots to look at your garden, you will also want to wander around and among the pieces, and you will, therefore, see the lighting from a variety of places. However, you cannot satisfy every need. The lights for one feature will, inevitably, impinge on another feature, so it is easier to think of a number of defined viewing points and to choose to light the garden from those points. Remember, too, that the viewpoints inside the house are as important as those outdoors.

If you want to see the garden from your terrace or deck, it is important to keep the lighting well balanced. The strong lighting within this covered deck makes it into a self-contained space, and not even the candle placed beyond it can serve to include the surrounding garden.

Decks and Terraces

Many gardens include a place to sit, which is usually adjacent to the house, even if it is not thought of formally as a terrace or patio. Often such a place forms naturally – it is where people gravitate instinctively when they are sitting in the garden. There may be more than one, and you would expect to find several in a larger garden. If the garden has been designed, either by yourself or a professional designer, these places may well have been formalized with paving or timber decking, but even if they are not, they can still be places used at night as well as by day. Even if you don't have a defined patio or a terrace or a deck, it will be worth while providing your sitting area with some light. Of course, if you have a patio in the original sense of the word – that is, a paved inner courtyard – you are likely to be living in a climate well suited for being outside at night, and lighting will be essential.

Whatever form your sitting area takes, the lighting will need to follow a number of similar guidelines. You will be sitting outside in your garden and so you will want to be able to see it, even if you also need to illuminate the terrace itself for some specific purpose, such as eating. The lights should, therefore, be kept below eye-level, and they should preferably be shielded by planting or some other means, so that they do not get in the eyes and cause glare. Lighting for secondary functions should take this into account and, ideally, have independent switching.

Low-level downlighters would be suitable, with perhaps some path-lighters dotted around the perimeter or among pots and planters. If you have decking with open slats, it might be worth trying to light it from underneath, although you would need good access or enough clearance to allow you to keep it tidy and gain access for maintenance. Benching provides an ideal place to put lighting for a deck or even a balcony, and lights placed underneath a bench, perhaps shining through the foliage of a pot plant, provide excellent, subdued illumination.

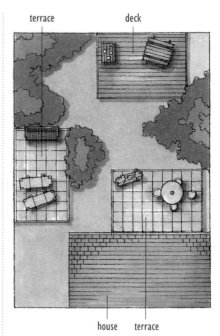

A large garden may have more than one sitting area, each of which will require its own lighting.

Two simple lanterns fit in beautifully with the style and feel of this terrace, and the cleverly placed mirror gives the illusion of much greater depth than really exists.

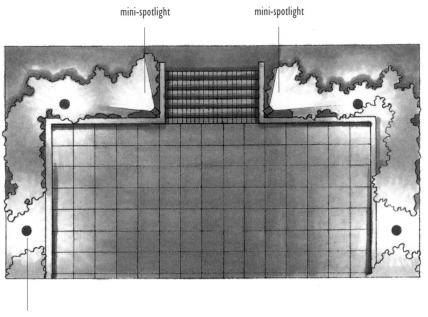

mini-spotlight   mini-spotlight

Low-level
perimeter
lighting is a
good choice for
a terrace.

path-lighters

Under-bench
seating will
minimize glare.

Bear in mind the impact that any local light will have on the view of the rest of the garden and avoid putting in any lighting that will eclipse the view, either because there is too much light or because it is inappropriately sited.

Remember, too, that the view from another spot in the garden should be taken into account. It may well be possible to combine lighting for the terrace with lighting for the house itself, thereby creating something to be looked at as well as something to be looked from.

For many people, the patio, terrace or deck will also be where they might have a barbecue or, at least, where they might want to sit outside for an evening meal, and this use carries its own problems. The special needs of eating areas are considered on pages 102–6, but, whether it is for a specific use such as eating or not, it is sensible to be able to control the lighting separately from the rest of the garden lighting, so install a local switching point if possible. Localized switching for something like eating is particularly important if the eating area is part of an extensive terrace, other parts of which might be used more like a pergola (see page 80).

Arbours and Gazebos

Garden structures such as arbours and gazebos can be thought of in a similar way to the patio or terrace. They are places in which to sit and look at a view, but they are, at the same time, features in their own right and, as such, are part of another view. As a result, it is important that a balance is achieved so that neither aspect overpowers the other. Whether you are dealing with a rose arch over a seat or bench or an Arcadian temple large enough to accommodate a string quartet, the principles are the same.

There is an increasing number of temporary canvas awnings available – open-sided tents, in effect – which are often described as gazebos. Many are offered with portable clip-on lighting, which usually takes the

Here the arrangement of lighting focuses exclusively on the imposing tree and garden building. Should you want to look out from the building you would have to consider a quite different arrangement to avoid being blinded by such powerful floodlights. The photograph shows the importance of colour and colour rendering.

Lighting an arbour.

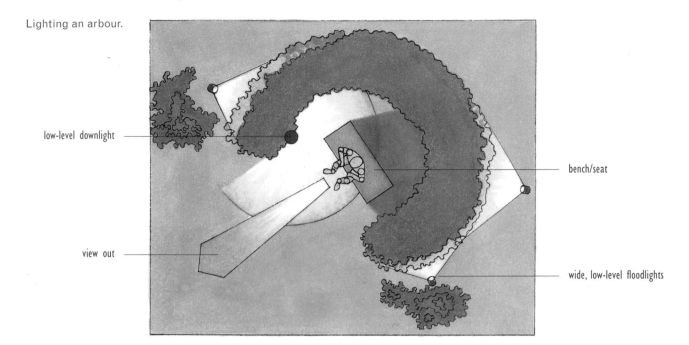

low-level downlight

view out

bench/seat

wide, low-level floodlights

form of globe lights arranged in a festoon for draping about at head height or as a group for fixing to a parasol pole. As temporary party and festive occasions they do an adequate job, but they are strictly temporary. I am more concerned with permanent structures in this section.

It is best to think of arbours, gazebos and so forth primarily as objects to be looked at and only secondarily as sitting places. Light them so that you can see their external features clearly. The lighting should enhance their shape or form or surface texture, but, because people might be sitting inside, avoid lighting from any level or point that might shine directly into the eyes of those within. Recessed uplighters placed around the outside would be ideal, particularly if you could conceal them among some low-level planting. It is possible to obtain fittings with special louvres designed to prevent glare, and they would be an excellent solution in these situations.

Internal lighting is more difficult, and much will depend on the scale of the feature in question. A simple rose arch may need nothing at all, but the more complex and larger the structure, the more some lighting might be desirable. If you decide that

you do want some, keep it low as you did on the terrace, or, if there is enough height, place a single narrow spot to throw a pool of light on to the centre of the floor. This can give all the light you need without spoiling the exterior effect and can be dramatic in itself. If you are fortunate enough to have a large structure, try putting high-level uplighters around the top to illuminate the inside of the roof – it works well in many a church.

If you have an old garden with genuine period features, you may wish to keep any lighting in sympathy with the original structures. In a garden house of this sort a pendent lantern can be the best answer, especially if you could find a period oil or candle lantern. Electricity will always be more conveneient but, if you use it, try to avoid pastiche – electric lighting is, after all, a modern thing and no one need be ashamed of the fact. This would be especially important for all those gardens that were designed by a professional landscapist with a strong personal style.

Above all, take care that any lighting does not obscure the view and make sure that there is something to look out at.

Uplighting a pergola.

Pergolas

Although the word has become somewhat diluted in its meaning over the years, a pergola is a covered walkway that is formed of growing plants trained over a framework of some kind. Often the framework or trellis is more apparent than the planting, but a pergola should feel like a green tunnel, through which glimpses of the world beyond may be caught. This is as true at night as during the day, and any lighting should take this into account.

It is probably best to think of a pergola as a path and light it accordingly with low-level path-lighters or recessed uplighters. If possible, conceal the uplighters to avoid glare, perhaps with louvres or by placing the luminaires among the ground-level planting as on the terrace.

The opportunity to downlight a pergola clearly exists and, provided they are narrow beams and sufficiently well spaced to leave dark intervals, this approach could work well. Downlighters may also be useful if there are features within the pergola, such as a statue, that could benefit from overhead lighting.

If you have seating within a pergola, you may want to provide it with some local lighting. If you do, install local switching so that it need be on only when it is required.

Seating within a pergola will, inevitably, be similar to that in an arbour, so you should consider the question of lighting in the same way. Provide enough for whatever specific purpose the light is intended, but not so much that it is not possible to see outside into other parts of the garden.

Orientation

Probably the most common reason for installing outdoor lighting is for orientation – that is, light by which we can see our way. Most municipal and much commercial lighting is done as much for this reason as for the spectacle itself.

Many people will put light outside their houses for themselves and their visitors to see by, even if they have no intention of providing lighting anywhere else. The main exception to this, of course, is lighting for security (see pages 116–19).

Orientation lighting can either mean the lighting of paths and walkways or directional lighting in parking areas and the like, or it can mean the placing of lights at strategic points so that they can indicate the general shape of the garden and how to get about within it.

This open-frame pergola creates visual interest through the use of perspective. This is reinforced by lighting the individual arches, while the view into the rest of the garden is preserved.

The route from the house out into the garden is lit well by the pair of downlighters that are set just below waist level.

These solar-powered lights give a low glow and they are intended to indicate the route rather than to illuminate the path.

Paths

Path-lighters will usually take one of two forms: low-level, shaded lanterns or illuminated bollards. Shaded lanterns are intended to provide actual illumination, casting pools of light over a limited area. Bollards, on the other hand, are primarily markers, and the light they cast is a secondary consideration. Bollards are mostly designed for large-scale situations such as car parks and driveways; relatively few are on a scale small enough to be suitable for a garden, although the kit-type, low-voltage lights available from garden centres are widely available. How many you need will, of course, depend on the path or route you are lighting. Is it straight or winding? Are there things adjacent that you or visitors might trip over? Does the path do double duty as a driveway? Remember, too, that a row of closely spaced low-level lights can themselves be an attractive feature.

On a small scale, a useful form of path-lighters are solar-powered orientation lights. These use solar power to charge up batteries, housed within the luminaire, which give off a glow after dark. They are not powerful – indeed, they do not give off light as such – but they do give enough light to mark the route. Their main advantage is that if you do not

These solar-powered bollards will give up to four hours of bright light or eight hours of dimmer light, giving you a choice of uses.

A very dramatic effect is achieved by burying these spots under a layer of gravel. They illuminate the plants while marking the edge of the path.

intend to install an entire system, they require no wiring and are consequently quick and easy to put in.

Apart from the practical side of lighting a path for convenience or safety, it can also be used, with or without an actual path, as a mechanism for drawing the eye in a particular direction. If you have a feature to which you wish to draw the viewer's attention, a string of path-lights to guide the eye can often support the lighting of the feature itself, especially if the feature in question is within a large space. You do not have to have an actual delineated path for path-lighters to serve their main function of guidance.

Steps

Steps are particularly hazardous at night, and if there is any likelihood that people will want to use them after dark it is essential to provide them with some light. They may get enough from an existing scheme or from the light within the house, but if there is any chance of accident, it would be as well to illuminate them in some way, particularly if it is a relatively long or steep flight. Under-step strips, path-lighters or bollards of an appropriate scale will all do equally well but it is important that, whatever light is provided for, steps should not emit glare.

If there is a good amount of planting close to the steps, it would be a simple matter to place small, compact spotlights at strategic points up the flight.

Bollards are an excellent means for lighting paths, driveways, courtyards or any other open space through which one might walk or drive.

Casting light sideways across the steps will pick out any surface variations in the stone or brickwork or any planting within the steps themselves.

Driveways

In a driveway the problem is as much about how to control the lighting as about the type of fitting to use. It is really a question of scale and how the driveway relates to the rest of the garden. A good way to light your driveway, whatever size it is, is by the headlights of your car – they are always there when you need them and they are only on when you need them. This doesn't solve the problem for pedestrians,

The edge of the driveway is lit by this traditional street lamp, positioned to mark the gate into the garden.

of course, and for the purposes of this book, I am assuming you may want to use more sophisticated means to illuminate the approach to your house.

Many people solve the problem with floodlights, often in conjunction with infra-red sensor switching, and there is no doubt that this works efficiently as a system and infra-red switches are useful. It is, however, a crude solution: the fittings are rarely attractive, and there are other problems inherent with automatic systems such as these (see below).

So what to use? Bollards are clearly ideal for the drive, although they are far from being the only solution. Several companies offer recessed lights, many designed to be driven over, that are intended specifically for use in drives and car parks. Such lights provide opportunities for some interesting light details, but because of the need for sufficient strength to support the weight of a vehicle, they are disproportionately expensive. Other solutions are wall-mounted downlighters, bollards or pole-mounted lanterns, similar to the typical street light. There is a fairly wide range of styles to choose from, including modern and reproduction 'antique'. Your choice will, of course, be governed by your personal taste and needs and the style of your home, but it will be constrained by the fact that many of the

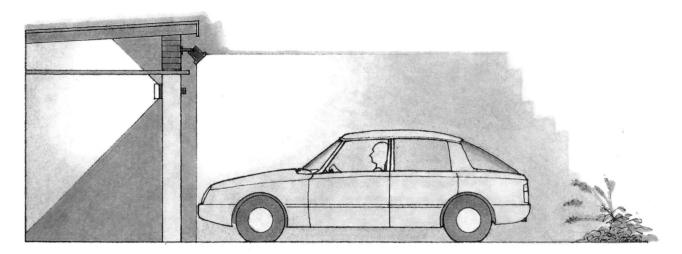

products available are designed for public spaces and are physically large and often expensive. Few companies offer modestly sized products, so you may need to shop around. A local wholesaler should be able to help, but, if not, the kit path-lighters of the sort mentioned above will do for small projects.

It is worth considering automatic switching or timed switching. Infra-red trigger switches can be placed so that the lights come on when they are needed, and, if they are combined with a timer to turn them off again, they are an excellent solution for drives and walkways; they are only on when there is someone to need them. But do be aware of the potential nuisance that can be caused if the control system you use is one of the relatively unsophisticated models – remember your neighbours and give them due consideration. If the lights go on and off too often, they could become a nuisance. It may be better to have some on all the time instead. Infra-red triggers could be a good solution in places that are used infrequently, and they are worth considering if your circumstances permit.

It may, of course, not be necessary to light a driveway directly. Lighting a row of trees or a bank of shrubs or a wall, for example, may well provide enough ambient light for the driveway. Lighting

A light or group of lights can be fitted with automatic switches that will sense the approach of a vehicle or the driver on foot. Most fittings of this kind will have a time delay so that the lights switch themselves off after a specified time.

objects around a subject is often a good solution, and this can be the best approach, especially if the subject itself is awkward to light for some reason.

Water

Before we leave the subject of path-lighters, there are places that might not immediately be thought of as paths but that, nonetheless, need lighting of this sort for the sake of safety. Open water is potentially dangerous at any time, but especially at night. If you have a swimming pool or a pond, putting path-lighters or bollards around the perimeter is a sensible safety precaution even if you do not intend to light the water itself. Of course, you will probably want to light the water feature anyway, especially if it has good detailing, such as a waterfall or fountain, but there may still be dark places where someone might be expected to walk, and a handily placed path-lighter may guard against such hazards. Water and water features are discussed on pages 89–99.

A beautifully planted small courtyard well lit by shielded downlighters combined with the traditional coach lamp above the door. Full advantage has been taken of the walls, and the light borrowed from the balcony adds an extra dimension.

SOME SPECIAL CASES

Courtyard Gardens

I want to make special mention of courtyards because, if they have been developed into a garden at all, they are often used as sitting and eating areas and are, therefore, particularly deserving of well-planned lighting. A small town courtyard garden is no different from any other form of garden. All the opportunities you might find in a large, extensive garden will exist or can be created, and it is often a case of just reducing the scale. The effects you can

produce will be no less interesting for being on a more intimate scale.

One of the aspects that defines a courtyard and that is, in fact, often the only difference between a courtyard and another form of garden, are the surrounding walls. They may exclude much sunlight during the day and, consequently, be regarded as a disadvantage, but they can be a distinct asset at night.

Walls will often have interesting surface textures and colours, particularly older brickwork, which will be picked up well by grazing the surface with obliquely placed spotlights or ground-level wall-washers. Even if your walls have trellis fitted to them, which is covered with mature climbers, grazing light adds drama to the space and provides a level of ambient light that would also be useful for orientation purposes. This effect works well on reasonably tall walls, where there is enough surface area to allow patterns of light and shade. It may be less appropriate on low walls unless the light source is focused to shine along the wall as opposed to up it. Clearly, projectors are best for this job, whether for high or low walls, and you could take advantage of adjacent planting to create shadow patterns, thereby enlivening even a smooth surface.

Another aspect of courtyards, as distinct from more open gardens, is that they are likely to be completely paved, with most of the planting being in raised beds or pots. These provide good subjects for lighting in themselves as they often have highly patterned and textured surfaces. A minor disadvantage with light in courtyards and, indeed, small gardens in general, is that, although it is possible to find all the light fittings you may need and to the appropriate scale, there are fewer manufacturers making them and there is, therefore, less choice. You may have to do a fair amount of hunting to find the fittings to suit your needs, particularly if you live in Britain. Don't give up – they do exist.

The Front Garden

In Britain especially, but certainly throughout much of northern Europe, occurs the phenomenon of the front garden. The classic front garden is a small patch in front of a suburban semi-detached or terraced house. It is often so small that it scarcely exists at all, being just enough to separate the house from the street. Larger houses, built later, may have enough space to park a car and have a flower border or two together with a patch of lawn. These are 'front gardens', intended as a declaration of private space and as a marker of increased opulence, albeit often on a modest scale.

Front gardens are rarely places in which one might sit, and, as a result, they are equally rarely considered as subjects for lighting. Yet there is a paradox here: because it is at the front of the house, the front garden presents an unequalled opportunity for showing off one's home, and what better way than to illuminate it at night. It is specifically these small gardens that I want to consider now; anything much larger can be treated in the same way as any other part of the garden.

Depending on the size of your front garden, a surprising number of solutions are possible. The simplest and most commonly used method is to install a pair of coach lamps or carriage lamps either side of the front door, or to put a downlighter inside the porch if there is one. Both of these techniques will serve to indicate the main entrance, to illuminate the route to it and also to act as a deterrent to intruders, and they are often all that is needed. Having said that, however, the front garden is one of the best places to use the low-voltage kits that are available from garden centres. They are easy and safe to install and are on the right scale for the circumstances.

More complex ideas include illuminating a small tree or shrub. You could even floodlight the front of the house, and this need not be as startling as it sounds. Using the appropriate luminaires, either to uplight from ground level or downlight from the eaves, would do the job and yet not be overpowering.

Whatever you are planning, in a very small garden, such as a courtyard, it is important to use luminaires of an appropriate size. Many of the fittings designed for use in commercial or municipal situations are large and would look absurd in a confined space, so whatever you use, keep them small. Remember, too, that the front garden is a semi-public place and you must take care to avoid the lighting causing a nuisance to neighbours or passing traffic. And sadly, you may have to make them safe from theft.

The Roof Garden

One of the main pleasures of a roof garden is being able to look out and enjoy the sense of being above it all. Being able to see a surrounding cityscape from the roof is a particular pleasure in itself, but being able to sit in a garden on that roof has a special feel.

It is important that the surrounding view is included in the design of the roof garden and that any lighting scheme takes this into account. Indeed, being able to see the stars is one of the greatest pleasures of sitting out at night.

Lighting a roof garden brings all the same opportunities and limitations of lighting a garden at ground level. The solutions I have discussed for ground-level gardens can all be used on the roof to good advantage. You may have to decide on your priorities at this point, but if your environment allows you to see the stars, it would be a shame to neglect them – include them if you can.

This generous balcony overlooks the city and takes advantage of the view at night as fully as it would by day.

WATER FEATURES AND POOLS

Designing the lighting for water and water features, like designing the
water feature itself, needs clarity of thought and intention. Of all the
things you can do in your garden, installing a water feature is, perhaps,
the most exciting, the easiest to get wrong and the most difficult to
change if you are dissatisfied with the results. Clearly, the larger the
feature, the more difficult it will be to carry out successfully, but size is,
in fact, of little relevance – it is no easier to design a small pond than a
large one. A formal water feature, built of brick or stone, with hard
landscaping and decorative fountains and falls, is often easier to make
than a more natural-looking pool – imitating nature convincingly
requires a special sort of skill. But if it is got right, the inclusion of water
in a garden can turn the mundane into the spectacular.

 Remember one important factor about water in the garden: whatever
your original intention, water will attract wild life – insects, weeds,

Lighting water can be a challenge, but
it need not be complicated; a single
light source may be all you need.
Here, a well placed side-light brings
out the form of the rock and catches
the water as it falls, throwing moving
shadows on to the rock behind.

frogs, dead leaves and so on will all find their way into your water, and, unless you are prepared for constant vigilance, it is wise to take this into account. And since the inclusion of wild life is almost inevitable, it would be as well to plan your pool and its lighting on that assumption.

The Nature of Water

To discuss the nature of water may not appear relevant in a book about lighting, but if you do not already have a water feature in your garden, it might be helpful to think about the sort of feature you want and, hence, the sort of lighting you might install to accompany it. There is no shortage of potentially good lighting effects, but not all will be suitable for all situations, and the sort of water you have has a direct bearing on the sort of lighting you provide.

Still or Moving

Water can be either still or moving – a pool or a stream. This sounds pretty obvious, but if you have a natural stream in your garden, it is likely to be the only constant form of flowing water you will have. In an artificial stream, the water will be still when the pumps are turned off, and if you have a stream with a continuous slope, there will be no water at all when the pumps are off. Conversely, a stretch of ostensibly still water, such as a pool, will have motion when even the slightest breeze blows; indeed, the times when it will be completely still are likely to be rare, unless it is a small pool in a well-sheltered position.

Natural or Artificial

The decision to have still or moving water may be influenced by whether or not you want it to appear natural or deliberately artificial. All man-made water features are, of course, artificial; in this context, I mean that it is built with no intention that it should appear natural.

The word pool implies still water, which, if it is to include motion, will need a waterfall or a fountain of some sort. Natural pools or ponds do not have fountains – at least, not in nature – so, if you wish to retain the illusion of nature, the decision between natural and artificial is made for you. The nearest thing might be a spring, but, even then, the fountain would have to be small – water, after all, prefers not to flow upwards. The illusion of a spring is best provided by a low-powered, well-submerged fountain head, so that the movement of the water only just breaks the surface, creating movement by ripple rather than by flow. If you want a proper fountain, you will have to opt for an artificial pool – there really are few things more absurd than a fountain in a natural pond. Natural water in motion is, therefore, best achieved by making a stream. It will, in fact, be a series of pools connected by weirs, with the motion created by pumping the water around in circles. There is a risk that it will look odd when you turn off the pumps, but this is unavoidable unless you are prepared to run the pumps continuously.

Deliberately artificial water, on the other hand, can have whatever you like, both of water effects and lighting effects, since there is no illusion to destroy. This widens the scope a great deal, and you can allow your imagination to run riot. It is the best choice if your primary goal is to create fantastic and fanciful moving water effects, and some of the major manufacturers have created some exciting products, not all of which need cost a fortune and many of which include an element of lighting.

Water features are, in fact, an excellent opportunity for using light for its own sake and, perhaps, the best for any special effects such as lasers or projections. Bear in mind, however, that special effects of this kind should be used with caution – remember that you are lighting the garden, not creating a theme park, and also that such effects are likely to be expensive.

Surface Lighting

If your water is intended to appear natural, you need surface lighting – underwater light will look as bizarre in a natural pond as a fountain will. A natural-looking waterfall will be best lit using surface lighting to pick up the motion of the water and the colours of the nearby rock and planting. Aiming a spotlight at moving water will cause the light to 'bounce' off the running water on to whatever is adjacent. 'Borrowed' motion of this sort is a good way to introduce animation into the garden, because it does not require any special luminaires. This method can be also easily exploited for water that is just moved by the wind.

Even if the surface of the water is moving, reflections will still look attractive. Avoid shining a light on to the surface of a still sheet of water; it will do little of any interest on its own. If you want to light a body of water in itself you should be thinking of underwater light.

A mixture of nature and artifice: this pool is clearly man-made even though it has been given an informal shape and naturalistic planting, and the submerged lighting serves only to increase the sense of artificiality.

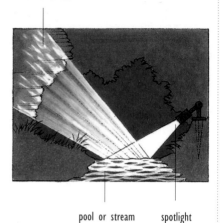

rock or shrub

pool or stream   spotlight

A spotlight aimed at moving water will cause the light to 'bounce' off the water's surface.

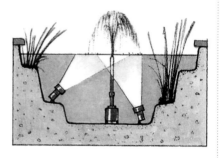

Install only luminaires that are specifically made for use underwater in a pool and always read the manufacturer's instructions. Many of these luminaires use the water as a coolant and should not be switched on until they are submerged.

Underwater

Submerged light is best used when a water feature is deliberately artificial, and in these situations the effects can be stunning. As with fountains, if the water feature is intended to appear natural or actually is natural, underwater lights will serve only to destroy the illusion. Having said that, several companies supply underwater lights, ranging in scale from the grand installation to a modest pool, and the results can be spectacular. Small, comparatively inexpensive kits are readily available in garden centres, and they are often packaged in combination with fountains or as a part of a fountain.

Still and Moving Water

One thing still water does extremely well, particularly at night, is reflect light. Any body of still water will become a mirror, reflecting anything adjacent to it. During the day this might be an overhanging tree, the passing clouds or a nearby building, even distant mountains, if you are lucky enough to have them and if the angle of view is correct. At night, the classic example of reflected light is the moon over the ocean, though most of us will have to settle for any adjacent local lighting.

The essence of surface lighting when the water is still is, therefore, reflection, and a lit feature seen from across a stretch of water is one of the most evocative of sights. Using water as mirrors is an ancient technique, much used by Zen gardeners. The idea was to create daylight reflections of rocks, buildings and planting, and night-time reflections of the light from the moon or stone lanterns. Sometimes known as 'mirror-lighting', the technique can be used in even the most modestly sized pool.

It is unlikely that you will have a lake with a Greek temple set romantically on the far shore, but you may have a particularly attractive planter or jardinière or a piece of sculpture, which would make an ideal subject for mirror-lighting. Even the planting on the other side of the water can be a suitable subject for mirror-lighting. If you are intending to give it light anyway, this will happen by default, so plan to include it rather than letting it happen by accident.

Illuminating an object placed beside a pool is one of the most beautiful effects that you can create when you are lighting still water, but a body of water is more likely to be moving than not, at least to some extent, and there are two ways in which you can exploit this motion: you can bounce light off the surface or you can shine light up

through the water itself. In both cases such light will move if the water does, throwing moving shadow and light on to an overhanging shrub or rock, painting the surface with a rippling, ever-changing pattern of light and shade, and producing attractive details. The ripples reflected on to a nearby rock will often catch the eye more readily than the waterfall itself.

An increasingly common effect is to float luminaires on the surface of the water. These usually take the form of internally lit globes, singly or in groups of two or three. They do not give a lot of light – indeed, they are not intended to do so – but they have an ethereal feel about them and can lend an otherworldly atmosphere to a garden. Fittings of this sort are made by the same people who make fountain kits, and they are designed to be a part of such an installation. They will, therefore, be low voltage, which makes them simple to install, and they are readily available in garden centres. They look just as good on their own as in groups, and they look equally attractive whether the water is moving or not.

Falls that are made to appear artificial give greater licence. These falls, though informally shaped, are none-the-less made to look 'built'; the submerged uplighting adds to the fantasy and enhances the drama of the pool.

Waterfalls and Streams

A natural or natural-looking waterfall is undoubtedly best lit with spots of an appropriate size put in concealed places so that the light sources are not visible (or, at least, not obvious) and are focused to catch the sparkle and splash of the water. Since they will, inevitably, be visible from somewhere, you should plan them in relation to a viewing point or points as much as to the waterfall itself.

Artificial falls give you more licence. You could treat them in the same way as a natural fall and to just as good effect, but they offer opportunities to be more adventurous. The very artificiality of the feature allows you to include colour and other effects that would be inappropriate to a natural waterfall. If you are planning the lighting at the same time as the design of the fall, you can include it as part of the

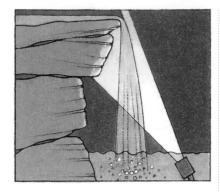

A waterfall can be either uplit or backlit.

A complex water course will require several light sources.

scheme from the outset. Adding to an existing installation will be less straightforward, but if there is sufficient space, try uplighting from the bottom of the fall by placing a submersible luminaire directly under the water as it hits the surface of the pool. If you have a feature in which the waterfall takes the form of a wide sheet, try back-lighting it as it falls with a strip of light under the lip or a luminaire positioned inside the structure.

If you have a broken fall or a number of small falls, try dotting it with sparkle lights. Tiny, low-voltage luminaires are available that are intended for underwater situations, and these are excellent for adding sparkle, but make sure you use a lamp of a power appropriate to the scale of the water feature. Fittings of this sort can carry lamps from between 5W and 20W – you will be surprised how much difference that will make in situations such as these.

If you have the resources, fibre optic lighting is ideal for this job, but it is expensive.

Whatever form of lighting you choose, remember that you don't want to dazzle the viewer, so make sure that the actual light sources are concealed.

The illusion of nature is deliberately broken here by the inclusion of the fossils and the submerged light at the foot of the fall.

An elegant, naturalistic fall is well lit by the side-light, focused to catch the movement of the water.

Fountains

The options for lighting fountains are similar to those for waterfalls, but fountains do offer special opportunities. They are, by nature artificial, and the sculptural element is often more important than the water. If you have a fountain within a pool it is most likely to be a jet or group of jets. Jet fountains are available off the shelf, and they often have lights built in or have lights as an optional, add-on feature, which you can buy separately.

If you want to install something more elaborate, look for one of the wide variety of decorative fountains available from water garden centres. Sculptural fountains are less likely to have integral lighting, so you will almost certainly have to design it yourself. You could concentrate on the object as a sculpture, leaving the water to add sparkle, or you could have a fountain with built-in lights, which are available in varying degrees of complexity, some being so complex that they require computer control.

This beautiful marble fountain, set in a formal pool, is lit with great drama from below the water. The uplight gives good modelling to the figures and brings out the quality of the stone.

A pair of uplighters gives drama and form to this wall fountain.

Approach a sculptural fountain in much the same way as you would a piece of statuary, with the aim of enhancing the shape and texture of the object (see pages 72–5). A fountain with built-in lights will probably be simply a matter of installation, since the manufacturer will normally have done the designing for you. A recent development, and one that is worth considering, is a fountain that uses the flow of the water to conduct a beam of light, in much the same way as fibre optics. Whatever their scale, and they can be large as well as quite intimate, this effect of shining light along, and within, a jet of water is beautiful to look at and gives a fascinating effect.

Remember that the installation of a sophisticated fall or fountain will not be straightforward. It will certainly require a specialist contractor, and you should consider seeking the advice of the manufacturers themselves since they often offer design and installation services.

Each gargoyle is cleverly lit from a concealed point under the lip of the pool, and there is sufficient ambient light from these three spotlights to illuminate the whole setting.

Bridges

Bridges do not necessarily cross water. They can be part of a dry feature as well as a wet one, and the Karesansui-style of Japanese garden – that is, dry mountain and water – will often include a bridge as an important element of the design. A bridge, wet or dry, offers a splendid opportunity for lighting.

Size is not the most important consideration. It is unlikely that lighting the superstructure would be appropriate in anything but the most extensive of gardens, but uplighting the underside of a bridge can produce dramatic results on any scale. The underside of a bridge offers the same opportunities for reflecting rippling movement as the adjacent rocks, and even on a small scale this is worth considering if you have a bridge-and-water combination that can be seen from a distance. An under-lit bridge can be a real eye-catcher.

If your bridge is part of a route around the garden or if you have stepping stones across a piece of water as part of that route, some form of lighting may be essential to preventing people from getting wet feet.

The lighting under this elegant bridge demonstrates just how effective underwater lighting can be. It makes it an attractive feature and provides light for those wishing to cross it at night.

Swimming Pools

It is a curious phenomenon that a great many domestic swimming pools are uninteresting, even unattractive, to look at. They are often – or, at least, they appear to have been – installed as if an afterthought, they are commonly a vivid blue in colour, and they are usually in sterile settings, devoid of life or interest. No amount of quirky shapes or clever lighting effects can truly make up for the intrusion of an ill-conceived swimming pool into what may be, in every other respect, an attractive garden. This is the more curious in cooler climates, such as in Britain's, where a swimming pool is probably in use for only one week of the year, and for the remainder of the time lies sullenly under a cover in an atmosphere of neglect.

It need not be so, however. There is no logic to say that a swimming pool may not be designed as an attractive object in its own right, in harmony with its surroundings, or that it may not be altered and enhanced so that it becomes so. If you are still in the planning stage, I urge you to think of the pool in the context of the rest of the garden, not as a thing in isolation. If you already have a pool such as I describe, there are several things you can do to improve the situation. Changing the shape would be a big undertaking, but changing its surrounds is a lot easier and lighting can help a great deal in integrating an obtrusive pool into the garden.

As with any other body of water, lighting a swimming pool is an important safety factor, so it is prudent to install some form of light, no matter what else you intend to do. It is probably necessary that a swimming pool be hard landscaped, at least in its immediate vicinity, so, if you already have a pool, you will need to lift the paving in order to install cabling, and you might as well take the opportunity to improve its appearance at the same time. If you are planning a new pool, now is the time to plan the lighting installation as part of a whole scheme.

The lighting along the steps, combined with the strong lighting in the doorway, combine with the water to make the most of this swimming pool. It illuminates the water's edge and also provides a dramatic view by exploiting the water as a mirror.

What you do with light will depend on the pool and its location. If it is visible from any of the viewing points we have already discussed, you should try to integrate it into the view. Another option is to surround the pool area with planting or screening of some sort to make it a discrete area, but, whatever you do, you should try to think about the lighting for its attractiveness as well as its inherent practicality.

Because of its nature, the swimming pool is an obvious candidate for underwater light – indeed, in warm climates, where the pool is often used after dark, it can be an important safety consideration. Think of the pool not only as something to be looked at but also as something to be used, and consider that it would be sensible to have two independent circuits to cater for these two aspects. One of these circuits will control the surface light, by which you can use the water for mirror effects, for example; the other will be for the underwater light to give a completely different appearance and for practical use.

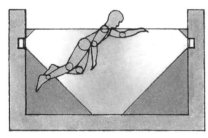

Submerged wall lights will provide an exciting glow in a swimming pool while providing adequate practical light for safety.

Planning your water

Below is a checklist of the sort of things you need to ask yourself when you are planning a water feature for your garden. It is included separately here because of the specialized nature of lighting water, but it should, of course, be part of your overall garden design or, at least, part of your lighting design scheme. It will be hard to include lighting after the event because you may have to get wiring close to the water or even into the water itself, and you will not want to disturb the lining and risk causing a leak. You will certainly not want visible, surface wiring – not only is it susceptible to damage and therefore dangerous, but it is unsightly. Remember that you may need planning permission – either for the water feature or the lighting, or both.

- *Is the pool to be formal or informal? A formal pool will, in effect, be unnatural and artificial.*

- *How large and complex will it be? Make sure that its size is in proportion with the rest of your garden. It could be tiny – a little detail in the corner – so don't ignore any possibilities.*

- *Will the water be still or moving? If you have a formal pool will it have weirs or fountains or both? Moving water in a natural pool will, of course, be provided by a fall and not by a fountain.*

- *If it is moving, what size pump do you need to use? Get expert advice on calculating the correct type of pump.*

- *Where should the pump be sited? Can you include the wiring for the lights in the same conduit?*

- *Will the lighting be surface or underwater? A natural pool should have surface lighting, and the wiring for surface lighting should ideally be included during construction. Underwater lighting can be built in or free standing or even floating – which will it be?*

- *Do you want to introduce colour? This will not affect the construction but it will influence the design. Keep to white for lighting all natural water features.*

- *What will be the effect on wildlife? Fish don't appear to mind a certain amount of light, but lighting up the night for prolonged periods may well upset other forms of wildlife, such as ducks and amphibians.*

SUMMER AND WINTER

So far we have considered the garden as a place for summertime, and, indeed, that is, I suspect, the way that most of us think about it. Apart from doing the routine maintenance work that all gardens require, few of us will venture out into the garden during the winter, the less so the harsher the weather we are likely to get. In some parts of the world this is not an issue, since the difference between summer and winter may be negligible, but for all of us who live in temperate climates, and in the right latitudes, the seasons have a profound effect on how we feel about our personal landscape and, therefore, how we use it.

No matter where we live, we should not let ourselves ignore our gardens during apparently unseasonal times of the year. Just because we don't want to be outdoors does not mean that we should forget to look at it. Anyone with a good view of the garden from a sitting room or conservatory, for example, can take advantage of that view whatever the time of year. Snow and frost transform the landscape, making the garden a magical place and bringing out quite different qualities from those that we see when the trees are in full leaf. We can learn another lesson from the Zen gardeners of Japan who understood this so well that they would include special snow-viewing features into their garden designs. Called *yuki-mi-doro* – the snow-viewing lantern – they are designed to catch the snow so that it may be seen and appreciated by the viewer.

The whole shape and bulk of the garden will change under a covering of snow, whether it be a light dusting or a thick blanket and, of course, if it looks good during the day, it can look spectacular by night. None of the lighting techniques we might use to light the garden during the winter will vary much from those we would use in the summer, and the same principles of shape, intensity and so on will apply equally well. But there are additional aspects to a winter garden.

The annual plants will have vanished – even the perennials will be dormant – so we are dealing more with large items, and many of them will have changed. Many conifers are natural snow-catchers, acquiring the most fantastic and outlandish shapes and outlines when they are covered with a bit of snow; in some areas they are grown deliberately to exploit this talent. Deciduous trees and shrubs will be naked and reveal quite different shapes and silhouettes, which benefit from lighting no less than when they were in full leaf. Remember, unless the snow is many feet thick, the heat from your luminaires will burn holes through the covering and the light they give out will be just as effective as in summer, albeit of a different quality.

Even those of us who live in areas where significant snowfall is rare, if it happens at all, are still likely to get a good frost from time to time, and frost can produce effects every bit as exciting as snow.

Many gardeners are aware of the garden at all times of the year and will have planned an all-season planting scheme to provide year-round interest. Several shrubs are grown specifically for their autumn and winter interest – dog wood (*Cornus* spp.) is often grown for its red winter bark, for example. An all-season garden is the ideal in any case, and if you have one or are planning one, you should certainly not neglect to light it for all seasons.

Water features, of course, can produce some of the most stunning and fascinating effects when they frozen. No one who has seen a frozen waterfall is likely to forget the sight; ice can make the most fantastic, outlandish shapes out of water and frost can create beautiful patterns on a sheet of frozen water. None of these possibilities should be ignored – all are excellent subjects for lighting. Remember that pumps and pipes can freeze in extremely cold weather, although moving water is less likely to freeze over than still water.

It is not just winter that brings its own special character to the garden; all the seasons have their

The fact that these plants are in their dormant winter state has been exploited here. The lighting brings out the tones of winter foliage just as well as it would those of summer.

own special accent. It may still not be warm enough to sit out in, but early spring has a freshness of colour that is quite different from the strong greens of summer, and autumn brings wonderful oranges, reds and browns, all of which look every bit as exciting at night as during the day. The colour and tone of the natural daylight will differ at these different times of the year, which is a phenomenon worthy of study if you want to understand the nature and business of light, even if you do not subsequently exploit these differences directly.

It is possible to overstate this business of seasonal change, especially as it will be irrelevant to some readers, but I am, of course, an enthusiast and I hate to see a possibility wasted. Suffice it to say that all the seasons have their own qualities, and if you were feeling that your lighting scheme would be used only in the summer months and might, therefore, not be worth doing at all, I hope that I have opened your eyes and encouraged you to change your mind.

EATING OUT

In many parts of the world eating outdoors is part of everyday life, especially in the evenings when the heat has gone out of the day and it is pleasant to sit out and relax under the stars. Even in temperate climates, eating and entertaining outdoors is becoming increasingly popular. Since most of us entertain most often in the evenings, it is likely that it will be dark when we do so, at least for part of the time. If you and your guests are going to get the best out of the occasion, it is important that the cooking and eating areas are well lit. 'Well lit', of course, is not synonymous with 'brightly lit' – there is no need for the lighting in these areas to be so bright or ill placed that it eclipses the lighting in the rest of the garden. Indeed, it is on these occasions that you are most likely to want to look at your garden after dark, and your lighting for eating should be planned, therefore, as a part of the overall scheme.

Where better for an alfresco meal on a summer's evening than this charming terrace?

Cooking

It is not necessary to include a cooking facility outdoors just because you want to eat out there; many of us have separate dining rooms and kitchens, and an alfresco dining room has no intrinsic need for an alfresco kitchen. If you do include an outdoor cooking area, however, it must be well illuminated. A barbecue is, for practical purposes, the same thing as a kitchen, and the same rules apply. You will have a cooking area and a preparation area, and you will want to be able to see what you are doing in both. If you have barbecues often enough to want a permanent installation, remember that practical, working light should come from somewhere in front of the cook or from the side, and it should be high enough to do its job but not so high that it gets in the cook's eyes. A wall-mounted downlighter would be ideal, or, if there is no convenient wall, you could think about trying a path-lighter instead. Many of these are designed as downlighters and would do the job admirably. A good cowled spotlight or a dedicated downlighter are the best choices for a barbecue.

If you want to light your barbecue infrequently, a temporary festoon of lights, similar to those used for parasol lighting would do the job well (see page 78). I have seen people rig up extension leads with table lamps and all manner of elaborate temporary arrangements, and I have often thought that they might just as well do something permanent and avoid all the hazards that temporary set-ups entail. You do not have to use electric lighting, of course. You could consider an oil lamp, but candles, although they are certainly fine for eating by, are not likely to produce a light that is strong enough to cook by.

Try to keep the cooking light local to the cooking place; you don't want it to spill over on to your eating area and certainly not to shine out over the garden, thereby limiting your appreciation of your surroundings.

Eating

If your barbecue is an outdoor kitchen, where you eat should be regarded as an outdoor dining room, and there is no reason it should be less comfortable or less convenient than your indoor dining room just because it is not in the house. Essentially, a dining place should provide enough light to see by without dazzle and without destroying the atmosphere. Many people, even those who cook outside regularly, day or night, fail to provide a good environment to eat in. It seems that, for many, the barbecue itself is the important part of outside catering, as if the activity of cooking were a more significant part of the occasion than the consumption of the food. My own view is that the eating and convivial conversation around the table are paramount, just as they are indoors. I have lost count of the number of times that I have attended outdoor festive occasions and been expected to balance my plate on my lap with nowhere to put down my glass (often losing it, or at least its contents, as a result). Quite apart from the discomfort this causes, it is impossible to provide light in such an *ad hoc* fashion, and the whole experience is more often a penance than a pleasure.

The modest electric lighting is well supported by a wealth of candles – an ideal temporary solution.

Assuming you want something more permanent than an oil lamp, effective though they can be, you will have to consider the design of the whole facility. Remember that it is an alfresco dining room and treat it as such. You should try to get the light in the same relationship to the table as it would be indoors – gentle overhead illumination and surrounding accent light.

Probably the best place for an exterior eating place, from the point of view of lighting is under a pergola, which can provide the necessary 'ceiling' for installing downlighting. The pergola can carry the central light, and peripheral light can be placed at ground level or under the benching if you have any. If you do have a pergola but you do not want permanent lighting, you might consider installing an exterior power socket into which you could plug temporary lighting – a table lamp brought from the house, for example. If you don't have a pergola, you may have a conveniently sited tree, which you could use in the same way. A possible solution is to use an arm, with a pendent downlighter fixed to it. The arm, which is attached at the correct height, swings out of the way against the wall when it is not needed. Creative ideas such as this are just what are needed in the garden when it comes to lighting. You could make this type of fitting yourself and it would cost little

Electricity is not the only answer: candles and oil lamps will give quite enough light of the right sort, and will be decorative in their own right.

A pergola is an ideal solution to lighting an outdoor eating area. Narrow spot downlighters can be mounted on the cross-beams and focused directly on the table beneath, an arrangement that will minimize light spill into the wider garden that might eclipse other lighting elsewhere.

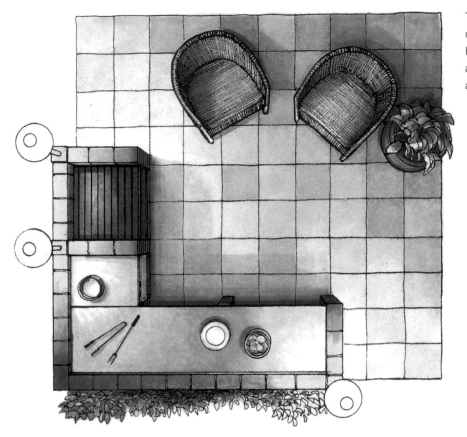

Three path-lighters have been mounted on top of the wall behind the barbecue and preparation surfaces, and make an ideal area for cooking and eating.

(although you must make sure you use exterior fittings and that you get a professional to connect it up for you).

There will, however, be places where downlighting will not be suitable. A pergola will not always be appropriate and sometimes it would be impractical to build one, or anything else, that could do the job satisfactorily. Here, side-lighting might be the solution. Carefully positioned path-lighters can provide good side-light for eating by, without glare or dazzle, as well as providing good local lighting for the terrace as a whole.

Should you wish to place your dining table in the middle of the lawn, unlikely though this sounds, then temporary lighting is going to be the only solution, and, unless you are prepared to risk trailing leads, it will almost certainly not be electric – and will be none the worse for that. Oil lamps and candles are the preferred lighting for many people for festive eating and parties, and they may be the only solution if you are able to provide neither electric downlight nor side-light.

For temporary lighting in these circumstances, take advantage of adjacent trees, structures or the like. You might use a garden sun umbrella to hold the light.

A portable clamp light in a conveniently sited tree.

barbecue

cooking light

patio doors

A large terrace or patio will require two-group switching to provide separate lights for the cooking and eating areas.

mid-level downlights

Parties and Events

Entertaining outdoors does not always mean sitting down to eat. Many parties and festive occasions might make good use of the garden as an overspill from the house. Of course, if it is the sort of party that includes or needs a marquee, then the company providing it will undoubtedly have temporary lighting rigs, designed specifically for the job. If you want to add to them, then there is all the opportunity you need in the form of garden flares and candles. Candle lanterns hung in trees are an ancient way of illuminating festivities that are no less valid today, although nowadays you might prefer to substitute a string of coloured lamps in their place, if only for convenience.

If your party and, indeed, your premises are on a less lavish scale, lighting the terrace is a useful way of providing overspill space for larger parties than can be comfortably accommodated indoors. For such an informal gathering there is probably no need for any formal seating arrangements, but a little lighting is essential, on the terrace at least, if it is not to feel like an annexe. Try to create the sense that it is a part of the house.

Switching

It is important to consider switching at an early stage, if only because of the extra wiring it might involve and the extra work that that will entail. You are not always going to want the barbecue lights on and that is equally true of the eating lights. There will be times when you might want to be able to isolate these areas from the rest of the scheme as well as from each other. If your cooking and eating area is on a terrace by the house, you will almost certainly want to keep its lighting independent. It is important that the lighting of these areas does not eclipse or obscure the view of the whole garden as seen from the house, and local switching is one way to ensure that it does not do so.

BUILDINGS

This book is primarily about gardens, but it would be a mistake to think that gardens include only trees, shrubs and water features. Many have an equal or greater emphasis on hard, built features than they do on plant life and all are, in any case, set within the

context of a house and its related buildings. These buildings themselves may be of sufficient architectural interest to merit illumination in their own right. In addition, the interface between the two may not be clear cut. The idea of bringing the garden into the house and, conversely, extending the house into the garden is becoming a more widely held idea, and not only in areas that enjoy warm climates throughout the year. We should not neglect the buildings when we are thinking about lighting our private piece of landscape.

The shapes in this lean-to conservatory have intrinsic interest, which is brought out nicely by the lighting. The use of glass here is intended to minimize the barrier between house and garden, and the balance of the lighting means that this will succeed just as well by night as by day.

Although the two are not mutually exclusive, we are dealing with two distinct ideas. First, we are thinking about bringing light to that area between the house and the garden so that we can make a continuous environment; second, we are thinking about lighting the buildings, either as whole things or detail by detail, as a part of a grand view. We will begin by thinking about the part between.

The Traditional Conservatory

A conservatory is a product of the eighteenth and nineteenth centuries and many houses dating from that time had one or, if it hasn't fallen down or been demolished, still have one. Adding a conservatory to newer property is becoming increasingly popular, particularly in cooler climates where they are used as a means of being outdoors while being protected from the elements. A conservatory is, in fact, just a glass room, and they were used traditionally for growing exotic plants, brought back by botanists and other enthusiasts from the 1700s onwards, and many people do still use them for this purpose. Most of these plants will be tropical or semi-tropical and they will need a good deal of heat and humidity. Any lighting put into conditions such as these should be waterproof, as should the switching, so think of it as a bathroom and put the switches on the outside – indeed it might be sensible to use exterior fittings even if they not strictly necessary.

If you have a conservatory that you use in this way, you might like to consider installing growth-enhancing lamps, such as are used by nurseries and florists. They are usually in the form of fluorescent strips and are intended to encourage vigorous growth, particularly among young plants. They do not, however, give a pleasant light to live by, so using them exclusively might restrict your use of the conservatory for other, less specialized purposes.

I suspect that most modern conservatories are used as an extra sitting room rather than for being used to grow specimen plants, and this will require quite different lighting.

The Conservatory as an Indoor-outdoor Room

The one thing that a conservatory can do really well is blur the boundary between the inside and the outside. It can bring the garden into the house and extend the house into the garden. In daylight this is comparatively easy. A well-designed planting scheme, inside and out, will achieve this, especially if it is combined with glazing in large sheets to cut down the amount of visible framework. But the effect is fragile and at night it can easily be lost. The problem is the glass. If you want to have light inside and still be able to see the garden, getting the balance right is of critical importance.

Lighting a conservatory is similar to lighting any reception room, although the emphasis is more on accent lighting than on practical lighting, but if we are going to pursue the idea of blurring the boundaries, bear in mind that any lighting indoors will tend to turn the windows into mirrors and will, to some extent, eclipse the lighting outside, and it is precisely that which we are seeking to avoid. We want to render the glass invisible, at least as far as that is possible.

A glazed lean-to will often be built to house a Jacuzzi or hot-tub, and there are few pleasures greater than sitting in a hot-tub at night and looking at the stars or out into the garden. You will need some light inside, if only to find your glass of wine, but the emphasis should be the light outside so that you lose sight of the glass as much as possible.

The best way to deal with the problem is to keep the light low to the floor and to conceal the light sources. Low-level downlighting, perhaps under benching or among planters, should be placed so that it throws shadow, rather than light, on to the glass. This should allow any light outside to be easily

visible from inside and will help to 'remove' the glass. It will certainly reduce the mirror effect.

Of course, you may want the space to have a bit more flexibility and to allow for more than just passively observing the garden. In this case, you should think about two distinct groups of lights, one to sit and look out by, and another for practical purposes. If you want to be able to use the space as an alternative sitting room or dining room from time to time, narrow, shielded downlighters should give you enough light while still preventing it from spilling on to the glass. You won't eliminate all the reflections, that would be impossible, but it should help. I suggest you experiment by moving small lights around to obtain the best compromise arrangement before committing yourself to a permanent installation.

The classic conservatory, well lit inside, is backed up by the illumination to the table. The concern here has been more to illuminate the areas of human activity than the garden within which it takes place.

The pools of light within the garden balance the lighting within the conservatory, making the juncture between the two less apparent. You would scarcely notice that you had changed from one environment to another.

A less happy arrangement where the garden is largely ignored.

The Garden Room

If your main sitting area is in a room with french windows or patio doors you could treat it in a similar way to the conservatory. Clearly you will need much more light in a sitting room or you would restrict its use too much, but you can take advantage of its relationship to the garden. Group pots, inside and outside, immediately next to the glass and conceal small lights among them. Keep the inside ones slightly dimmer than those outside, if possible. Again, you won't eliminate the glass altogether and the effect will be different from that in the conservatory, but it will go a long way to help.

If your sitting room or conservatory is planned to be one of your main viewing points for looking at the garden at night, this technique will be helpful, but do experiment. Remember it is the balance that will determine the best results. The side of the glass with the brightest light will become the mirror.

The Garden House

Many people have a garden house of some sort. It need not be an elaborate affair, a deck with a lightweight roof would class as a garden house as much as any grander construction. If you have a summerhouse or any garden building it will, almost by default, become one of your main viewing points, provided it is not just a shed (though even that might be convertible). If you have one that you use in conjunction with a swimming pool, to change in or to keep food and drink in, then you are just as likely to want to use it at night as you do the pool. And if you still want to see the garden, you will have the same problems as you did in the conservatory.

An open-air structure, such as a gazebo or an arbour, can be lit easily (see pages 78–9), but the moment you introduce glass you create a lighting problem. Glass will become a mirror unless you control carefully the position of the light sources and the balance of the light. Again, you should keep the light at or near ground level, and shield any light sources so that no light shines directly on to glass. And again, you should make sure there is no more light inside than there is out.

Carefully balanced uplighters on either side of the glass brings the garden indoors by effectively removing the glass. The outdoor lights should be brighter than those indoors, and take care that no light spills onto the glass itself.

Installing a concealed strip light below a windowsill, combined with the strong uplighters in the garden, has the effect of removing the glass altogether. The reflection from a reading light can be screened by, perhaps, a tall plant.

Architecture and Architectural Detail

The outside of your house is just as much a part of the garden as are the trees, shrubs, water features and so on, and it can often be an interesting object to light in itself. Just as many public and commercial buildings are floodlit at night, so can your home be – it doesn't have to be grand or old, almost any building will have some feature of interest that can look great at night with the right lighting.

If you are fortunate enough to have a home of particular architectural interest, and you do decide to light the outside, there are a number of ways in which the installation should differ from a similar project for a commercial or public building. You are living in the building so you will not want the light to shine directly into any of the windows. Clearly the light has to hit the house, so you cannot conceal the light sources entirely from view but you should aim to minimize the impact. This will be a compromise. The closer you can get the luminaires to the walls the better for minimizing glare, but the more difficult it will be to light the whole structure.

Try to strike a balance with the distance, and place the uplighters between the windows rather than underneath them. If you have an appropriate building, setting downlighters into the eaves is a good solution, but the eaves do have to be fairly deep and don't forget the heat that will be generated in what will inevitably be a confined space; the luminaires may need to be ventilated.

It is not necessary to light the whole structure, of course. Much will depend on the complexity of the style, but the architecture of the house may not stand up to full illumination. An alternative and possibly better way may be to bring out the details. Even the most modest of buildings will have some detailing that would make a good subject for lighting, or that could be lit in such a way as to give it more visual interest than it really has.

Small, tightly controlled spotlights can be used in

A traditional outdoor lantern. This is excellent for general illumination in the right circumstances.

a variety of situations around a building, and they will often give a much more interesting and subtle result than large floodlights will ever do. They should be placed so that they pick up the modelling of the detail in question or so that they graze the brick or stonework in much the same way as discussed for garden walls and screens (see pages 71–2). Remember that plain, rendered walls with sharp corners make excellent projection screens.

To light details you will have to take a long hard look at your house. Make an inventory of its most attractive or quirky features and start your planning from there. Good subjects include the porch to the main front door, an elaborate chimney, an interesting corner, an archway or a window reveal. If you are clever, you may be able to illuminate the whole structure with the combination of these details, although achieving this successfully will require a careful balance of wattage, beam width and distance.

Porches

A porch is a good place to start, since it will tend to be a focal point by default, and a downlight inside might be all you need. Think about how you use the light – being able to see the lock would be an obvious bonus, but it need not be by overhead light. Strip-lights beneath a shelf at waist height would do the job without creating glare or inappropriate overemphasis. If your porch is constructed on a grand scale, with columns and a pediment, you should treat it in much the same way as any other garden structure. Try strategically placed uplighters at the foot of columns or pillars, either on the outside or set into the floor on the inside to cast light up the structure and up towards the ceiling.

Corners and Angles

Many buildings, while not necessarily of special architectural interest, have interesting corners and angles. This is especially true of buildings dating from more than one period, which have been added to over the years, sometimes fairly indiscriminately. You might, for example, highlight the point where the roof meets an extension or where it is pierced by a chimney. Corners and angles created by additions and alterations make good subjects for lighting. Use uplight or downlight here, whichever is the more suitable for the specific circumstances, but try to place the luminaire so that the beam will pick out the feature to its best advantage. Don't forget the shadows that will be cast and think how you can project them on to an adjacent feature or wall.

Arches

Arches, whether they are part of the building or are free-standing structure, are often lit as part of grand public schemes. Yours may not be on the same scale as, for example, the Arc de Triomphe in Paris, but it will still make a good subject for lighting. Formal arches are rather like bridges in that they are often best lit from below to emphasize their height, which makes them appear grander than they really are. The same is true for arches that are part of a building.

Uplight confined within a shallow arched feature will bring out its form and change the whole feel of the wall that contains it. An arch through a wall or a

The arches are a strong feature during the day with good texture. The lights here will illuminate the immediate area but will do little to bring out the strength of the feature. Adding uplight within the arches, with the light sources concealed by the planters, would be better.

hedge is a point of conjunction, marking the point where one area stops and another starts. The right lighting can exploit this for dramatic effect, and if you get the balance right you can draw people towards and through the arch as if into another land. Providing strong lighting for the view through the arch and putting small, low-level uplights on the viewer's side will help achieve this and, with care, it can be just as successful the other way around.

Windows

The technique of confined uplight also works well for window recesses. You should take care that the light source doesn't create glare, but try a suitably baffled strip light along a windowsill or a pair of miniature spotlights, one each side of the frame, either focused to cross each other or to shine straight up the inside of the window reveal. Much the same result would be achieved by placing the lights on the inside of the window – it would, inevitably, be different but need not be any the less interesting. There is an added advantage, also, in that you can use micro-track inside, which means much more discreet luminaires, and you can exploit the sparkle inherent in unshielded dichroic lamps.

Although simple, the architecture of this house is very emphatic. However, the exterior lighting is modest and does not really do it justice.

Gates and Entrances

If you have an impressive entrance to the garden, perhaps some wrought ironwork or a timber lych gate, you should definitely think of illuminating it, because such structures make excellent subjects for lighting. Apart from announcing your entrance the better to your visitors, however, a well-lit gateway can make a fine spectacle in its own right. All the same rules apply as for any other garden structure, but you must take care that the lighting does not

We are left in no doubt where the doors are here, or which one the owner would prefer to be used.

interfere with the passing traffic or cause a nuisance to your neighbours.

If the gate is not of particular interest in its own right but you still want to illuminate the entrance, you should think about what you can use around it. Indirect light is no less effective than direct light would be, and lighting any adjacent trees, or other large planting, might well provide, indirectly, ample illumination for your entrance. You could try grazing the surface of the drive with low spots or install recessed drive-over luminaires into the surface to act as directional beacons.

One detail that is often overlooked: if you have powered gates operated from a keypad or an entry-phone of some sort, provide it with a light if it does not already have one built in.

This simple installation answers several problems with one light source. The doorway is well illuminated, the approach to the house is clearly defined, and the light gives the house a spectacular appearance at night.

SECURITY

People are increasingly feeling the need to install security systems to their homes, and a large element of these systems is some form of anti-intruder lighting. If your need is for a sophisticated system with all the trimmings, then you should consider consulting a security specialist who will be able to design and install such a system, and this will certainly be true if security is of more importance to you than making the grounds around your house interesting to look at after dark. But it would be a shame to miss the opportunity.

The needs of security can be satisfied by the garden lighting: the exterior lighting here would make this house extremely difficult to approach without being seen. However, it is important to consider the needs of the environment, in which case this solution may not be ideal.

Most of us, however, do not have such a pressing need and can be a bit more relaxed in our approach. It is, of course a fundamental truth that all security installations are, ultimately, just a deterrent. Really determined intruders will get in if they really want to, and you should, therefore, consider any anti-intruder system in direct relation to your real needs. It has even been suggested that obtrusive security systems merely announce that you have something valuable to protect, thereby encouraging the attempt. You should not, of course, be blasé about security, and it would be irresponsible of me to suggest any such thing, but this book is about lighting your garden, and our aims are to introduce subtlety and drama and create atmosphere and interest. Nothing is more likely to destroy these effects than powerful anti-intruder floodlights suddenly snapping on and drowning your carefully thought-out effects.

Lighting is an important part of any security system, but it should be included as part of an holistic approach to the entire scheme. It is perfectly possible to integrate lighting for security into your other garden lighting in one way or another. Bear in mind, too, that security lighting should include the lighting indoors as well as out.

Assuming that your aim is to try to integrate your security needs with recreational lighting, there are three main options:

- Automatic or manual switching
- A discrete system or borrowed light
- Dark-hours lighting or short-term light

This is something of an artificial division but it is useful for the purposes of this discussion.

Automatic or Manual Switching

Automatic or manual switching is probably the least important of the three, but we will consider it first because your selection will affect your other choices.

Any security system should be well planned. Make a scale plan of your house and garden so that you can easily identify walkways and potential dark spots.

If the security lights are turned on and off manually, the only problem is deciding where to put the switch, and that is a matter of finding the most convenient place or places. Of course, manually controlled security lighting is something of a paradox: lights that can be controlled only if you are at home. Automatic switching of some sort is the only answer for security, because it will work when the house is empty.

There are three possible solutions:

- A time switch
- A light-sensitive switch
- An infra-red trigger switch

Time Switch

The only drawback to a time switch is the variable length of the day in temperate climates. This is not an insuperable problem, but you do have to keep an eye on the time of year, and, of course, the regularity of a timer can limit its effectiveness.

Light-sensitive Switch

A light-sensitive switch is, in effect, a solar-powered time switch. It seems, at first glance, an ideal solution – you install it and forget about it. But unless you also install a means to limit its duration, such a switch will mean having the lights on all night. This is known as dark-hours lighting and, as far as it goes it is effective, but it does have inherent problems (see opposite).

Infra-red Trigger Switch

Infra-red trigger switching is excellent, provided you install switches to control lights as part of an overall

scheme and not just the light-with-switch kits that are available from many D-I-Y stores, useful though they are in certain situations.

Discrete or Borrowed Security Light

Borrowed security lighting – that is, doubling the use of some of the existing fittings as security lights – would be a good and economical approach in that it extends the use of some or all of your lights. There are difficulties, however, among which is the fact that the lights themselves may not be best placed for this secondary task, so you would have to select the least inappropriate and use them or install some extra ones for the purpose. Borrowed security light is worth considering, but it is not an ideal solution.

A better answer would be to install lights that are dedicated to the security system and are independent of the main lighting installation although they are designed as part of it. If this is the chosen solution,

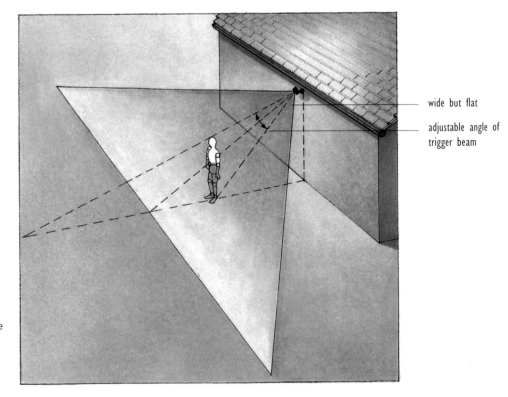

wide but flat

adjustable angle of trigger beam

The beams of infra-red motion or heat-detecting light sources are often very wide but flat, although adjustable ones are available to suit your particular requirements.

there should be one group, or a series of groups, activated by infra-red triggers on separate circuits from the other garden lighting. But make sure they are integrated and are a part of the overall design.

Dark-hours Lighting

The expression 'dark-hours lighting' means that the security lighting comes on at dusk and goes off at dawn, and should do so even while the house is unoccupied. It can be automated by timer control, or by installing light detecting switches, such as those used for street lights and lights in other public spaces, which are readily available from wholesalers. On the face of it, dark-hours lighting would seem to be a good solution, but it does have several environmental implications.

If you do consider dark-hours security lighting and you do not have a problem with it interfering with the rest of the garden, you should consider using bulkhead luminaires with compact fluorescent lamps. They use less power to run and have a long life span, and they are ideal for circumstances like these. Remember that it is better to put more lights in unobtrusive places than fewer lights in obvious ones, and keep the wattage low – you do not need a powerful light, just enough to see by. Fluorescent lamps of between 9W and 13W should be ample.

Short-term Automatic Lighting

Some means of controlling just the lights you want when you want them would be the ideal solution, and the best means to do this is to use infra-red triggers. The triggers could be part of a borrowed light system, controlling certain parts of your overall installation and doubling them as security lighting even when the rest of the system is turned off, or they could control dedicated security lights that have been integrated within the overall scheme. Using luminaires to double as garden and security lighting

sounds a good idea, but the wiring would, inevitably, be much more complicated, involving many more runs of cabling, making it expensive to install.

All things considered, we are left with the solution of fitting an independent security lighting system, integrated within the overall scheme, and controlled by infra-red triggers with automatic reset facilities.

Night-time Lighting and the Environment

Keeping lights on all night can be expensive to run, and it can play havoc with the natural cycles of the local wildlife. With the recent increase of triggered security systems, this is now becoming a problem in both town and country. Night-time security lighting is a compromise between the interests of security, your pocket, a recreational lighting scheme and the environment. Neither recreational lighting schemes nor the environment benefits from a great flood of light and, apart from the nuisance it can cause to yourself and your neighbours (both human and animal), there is no certainty that it will provide any greater degree of security than a well-thought-out and much more subtle installation, incorporating a mix of the ideas we have already considered. A number of lower-powered lights placed in carefully selected positions, such as above doors and in exterior passageways, will do a more thorough job than one high-powered floodlight. Several lights are more likely to deter intruders and will better satisfy the needs of your recreational scheme and of the environment.

A final word: I have long believed that infra-red trip switches would do a more useful and considerably less anti-social job if they were installed in strategic places around the garden but were wired to control lights inside the house. Even stereo systems or television sets could be part of such an installation, and together they would raise considerable doubt in the mind of a potential intruder.

GLOSSARY

A

All-round-glow A lamp designed to emit light evenly in all directions.

B

Bayonet clip (BC) or **bayonet base** A means of fixing a lamp into a lamp holder by means of two lugs. Known in the USA as a bayonet base.

Barn-doors The flaps mounted in front of a spotlight or floodlight to control the direction of the beam.

Beam Light that is directed in a particular direction. The beam from a lamp is classified by its diameter, a beam under 30° being a narrow beam and one over 45° being a wide beam.

Bollard A luminaire in the form of a short post with a lamp in the top. Such luminaires are most often used in car parks and as street furniture.

Bulb The glass envelope that contains the filament. See also LAMP.

Bulkhead luminaire A wall-mounted luminaire that is protected by a grille.

C

Central pendant A single or multiple lamp holder suspended from the ceiling of a room or other structure. The most common form of basic domestic lighting.

Coach lamp Originally, a luminaire that was fitted to a horse-drawn coach or carriage. Converted carriage lamps and reproductions later became popular for lighting either side of the main entrance to a house. Nowadays, any luminaire so placed, which is not specifically a bulkhead luminaire, tends to be called a coach lamp.

Colour of light The range of colours in the visible spectrum, from red to violet, which combine to make white light. Each constituent colour has its own wavelength.

Conduit A tube intended to carry electrical wiring and protect it from damage. For outdoor use a conduit is usually made of copper or steel. It can also be flexible, when it is known as a Greenfield connector.

Cowl A cover for a lamp that can either make a projector out of an all-round-glow lamp or that hides the light from a projector from most angles, thereby reducing glare.

D

Depth of field Usually a photographic term, meaning the relative distance of objects in focus from the camera. In lighting it refers to the power output of lamps at pre-determined distances relative to the viewer.

Dichroic reflector A multi-faceted glass bowl that is coated so that it projects light forwards and conducts heat backwards.

Dimmer A mechanical or electronic device for controlling the output of a lamp or group of lamps.

Downlighter A luminaire intended to shine downwards only.

E

Efficiency In lighting, energy efficiency is the ratio of light output to electricity consumption.

Edison screw (ES) Designed by Thomas Edison, the second most common means of connecting a lamp into a lamp holder. One contact is a button on the base; the other is the screw-thread itself. Known in the USA as a screw base.

F

Fibre optics A system of projecting light down the length of an optical glass fibre or bundle of fibres.

Filament A fine piece of wire through which an electric current is passed, causing it to glow white hot and give off light. See also LAMP.

Filter A sheet of glass or plastic that intercepts light from a lamp; it is commonly used to provide colour.

Floodlight or **flood** A lamp whose beam exceeds 45° diameter or a combination of lamp and reflector that achieves the same result.

Fluorescence The result of causing something to absorb invisible radiation and emit visible radiation. A phosphor coating on the inside of a tube or bulb is made to fluoresce, or glow, by ultra-violet radiation from mercury vapour.

Focal point The point or points in a field of view that are contrived to catch the eye.

Focus The adjustment of eye or lens to produce a clear image. Also, the concentration of a beam of light to within desired parameters.

G

Gel A piece of heatproof coloured plastic sheeting that is placed over a light in order to project colours. Gels are used especially in theatre and film lighting.

Gobo A disc of a metal, usually aluminium, out of which a pattern is cut. Used singly or with a colour filter, the disc is mounted over a spot projector.

Growth-enhancing lamp A fluorescent tube, often with pink-tinted glass, designed to emit wavelengths of light that will promote growth in plants.

I

Incandescence The result of causing something to glow white-hot; the principle behind the electric light-bulb, in which a carbon or tungsten wire (the filament) has an electric current passed through it.

Infra-red The hot, red end of the spectrum, invisible to the human eye.

Intensity The level of output from a lamp, measured in lumens and lux.

L

Lamp A light source, as opposed to a luminaire, which is made to carry a lamp. A lamp is composed of a bulb, a filament and a base.

Light The medium of illumination emitted by a lamp.

Light strings A length of wire to which lamp holders are fixed at predetermined intervals. Also a length of plastic, translucent tube into which lamps are fixed at predetermined intervals. Certain forms of both are often controlled electronically, enabling them to flash or light in pre-set sequences.

Lighting track A linear power socket to which luminaires can be fixed at any point along its length. The track is available in many forms, in both mains and low-voltage.

Louvres An arrangement of parallel bars placed across a beam to send it in a particular direction or to shield it from certain directions.

Low voltage A level of power stepped down from mains voltage by means of a transformer. Many luminaires are designed to operate at a reduced level of voltage, commonly 12V or 24V.

Lumen (lm) The unit by which the output of a lamp is measured.

Luminaire Any device designed or made to carry a lamp holder. As a rule, it includes lamp, lamp holder, body and any accessories such as reflectors or lenses but, at its most basic, a luminaire can be just a lamp and a lamp holder.

Lux (lx) The number of lumens per square metre.

M

Mains voltage The voltage level supplied by an electricity supply company. It is usually 220V or 240V in Britain, and 110V in North America (doubled for large appliances).

Micro-track A miniaturized version of a lighting track.

Miniature spotlights Specific types of small luminaire designed to carry a projector with a small cap size.

P

Parabolic aluminized reflector (PAR) A heavy glass enclosed projector lamp with an internal parabolic reflector, often with a lens moulded into the front of the bulb.

Path-lighter A luminaire specifically designed to illuminate a path, often designed to shine downwards only.

Projector A lamp designed to throw its light forwards in a controlled beam. Also an apparatus for projecting rays of light or projecting an image on to a suitable surface.

R

Recessed uplighter A luminaire, its body buried in the ground, intended to shine upwards only.

Recessed path-lighter A luminaire, its body buried in the ground, specifically designed to illuminate a path.

S

Spectrum The colour range of visible light observable when a beam is split with a prism.

Spotlight or **spot** A beam of light with a spread of less than 35°.

Stepped-down power Low-voltage power that is achieved by passing mains voltage through a transformer.

T

Task lighting Lighting that is designed to illuminate a specific task or activity.

Tone The quality of emitted light.

Tungsten filament A filament made from tungsten wire.

Tungsten halogen A lamp made of fused quartz glass filled with halogen and argon; it achieves grater energy efficiency than a standard tungsten-filament lamp.

U

Uplighter A luminaire intended to shine upwards only.

V

Volt (V) The unit of electrical potential by which current is measured.

Voltage drop The diminution of voltage between two terminals when current is taken from them.

W

Wall-mounted path-lighter A luminaire designed to be fixed to a vertical surface and intended to shine downwards only.

Wall-washer A luminaire designed to illuminate vertical surfaces, by means of angled uplight or downlight.

Watt (W) The unit of power (equivalent to 1 joule per second) used to describe the output of a lamp.

Wattage The output rating of a lamp.

INDEX

ACKNOWLEDGEMENTS

Jonathan Buckley 84(b); **Commercial Lighting Systems** 25; **Eric Crichton** 103 (Design: Angela Kirby); **Liz Eddison** 8–9 (Gavin Landscaping, Chelsea 1996), 31 (Agriframes, Hampton Court 1998), 32 (Chelsea 1996), 65(bl) (Agriframes, Hampton Court 1998), 70 (Natural & Oriental Water Gardens, Hampton Court 1997), 89 (Natural & Oriental Water Gardens, Hampton Court 1997), 94 (Natural & Oriental Water Gardens, Hampton Court 1997); **Garden Picture Library** 1 (Ron Sutherland/ Design: Anthony Paul), 15 (Ron Sutherland/Design: Anthony Paul), 43 (Sunniva Harte), 49 (Steven Wooster), 54–55 (Ron Sutherland), 64 (Ron Sutherland), 65(t)(Ron Sutherland), 66 (Jane Legate), 71(t) (Ron Sutherland), 101 (John Neubauer/Design: Oehme van Sweden & Associates), 110(t) (Ron Sutherland/Design: Duane Paul Design Team), 110(b) (Gary Rogers); **Jerry Harpur** 7 (Design: Victor Nelson, NYC), 10–11 (Design: Simon Fraser, Middlesex), 76 (Design: Mel Light, LA), 82(t) 11 (Design: Simon Fraser, Middlesex), 84(t) (Design: Mel Light, LA), 102 (Design: Hank Lith and Rod Taylor, Cape Town); **Hozelock Ltd** 39, 54. **Intersolar Group** 82(m), 82(b). **Keith Metcalf's Garden Heritage** 2–3, 44(t), 44(b); **Clive Nichols** 13 (Garden & Security Lighting), 12 (Garden & Security Lighting), 14 (Garden & Security Lighting), 16 Garden & Security Lighting), 28 (Garden & Security Lighting), 30 (Garden & Security Lighting), 52 (Garden & Security Lighting), 65(br) (Garden & Security Lighting), 72 (Design: Darren Yeadon, Hampton Court), 75 (Design: Emma Lush), 83 (Garden & Security Lighting), 91 (Garden & Security Lighting), 93 (Garden & Security Lighting), 95(tl) Garden & Security Lighting), 95(tr) (Garden & Security Lighting), 95(b), 96 (Garden & Security Lighting), 97 (Garden & Security Lighting), 104 (Design: Emma Lush), 112 (Design: Claus Scheinert); **Noral Ltd** 113; **© Stapeley Water Gardens Ltd. UK** 41;**Elizabeth Whiting & Associates** 29 (Michael Dunne), 34, 47 (Gary Chowanetz), 48–49 (Jerry Harpur/Design: John Vellam), 57 (Andrew Kolesnikow), 58 (Jerry Harpur/Design: John Vellam), 71(t) (Jerry Harpur/Design: John Vellam), 78 (Mark Nicholson), 81 (Andrew Kolesnikow), 86 (Michael Dunne), 88 (Tim Street Porter/Design: Barry Sloane), 98–99 (Tim Street Porter), 107 (Richard Davies/Design: Rick Mather), 109 (Steve Hawkins), 114 (Tim Street Porter/Design: Barry Sloane), 115(t) (Tim Street Porter), 115(b) (Clive Helm), 116 (Friedhelm Thomas); **Christopher Wray Lighting** 18, 19, 22, 23(l), 23(r), 24, 59, 61.

Keith Metcalf's Garden Heritage, Manor Road Nursery, Manor Road, Milford-on-Sea, Hampshire, SO41 0RG.

Noral Ltd, 26 Vincent Avenue, Crownhill, Milton Keynes, MK8 0AB.

Christopher Wray Lighting, 591–593 King's Road, London, SW6 2YW.